D1274073

## DATE DUE

| 5-4-05 | | | |
|---|---|---|---|
| | | | |
| | | | |
| | | | |
| | | | |
| | | | |
| | | | |
| | | | |
| | | | |
| | | | |
| | | | |
| | | | |

# STRUCTURAL FUNCTIONS
## OF HARMONY

# STRUCTURAL FUNCTIONS OF HARMONY

*By*

(Schönberg)

ARNOLD SCHOENBERG

*Revised Edition with Corrections*

*Edited by* LEONARD STEIN

W · W · NORTON & COMPANY · INC · NEW YORK

Library of Congress Catalog Card No. 74-81181

# CONTENTS

# CONTENTS

# ACKNOWLEDGEMENT

I HAD been constantly dissatisfied with the knowledge of harmony of my students of composition at the University of California, Los Angeles. To remedy this shortcoming I instituted a new class to which the conventional harmony teaching should be the prerequisite: STRUCTURAL FUNCTIONS OF HARMONY. At this time (1939) a young former student of mine, Leonard Stein, had already become my assistant and remained in this capacity for the next three years. Thus naturally when I started to write the present book I could not select one better to help me express my ideas. He had observed the development of these ideas from the very beginning and had watched me struggling with their formulation.

I was not wrong in this selection. While perhaps a perfectionist might have tortured me with corrections of my English, upsetting the flow of ideas, he had the patience to let me pronounce my sentences in their rudest forms if only they expressed the idea clearly. Of course the gravest grammatical errors had to be eliminated, but the polishing of the style could be postponed.

In spite of the preliminary work done in classes and Mr. Stein's collection of notes and examples at this time, the real writing and frequent rewriting of the book demanded nearly two years. The extreme number of examples necessary for illustrating and clarifying every problem; the application of the theories in the analysis of the examples from literature and the inevitable work of writing and copying are indications of Mr. Stein's share in the production of this book.

I use with pleasure this opportunity to thank him for his intelligent, careful, assiduous and discriminating assistance.

ARNOLD SCHOENBERG

28 *March* 1948

# PREFACE TO
# THE REVISED EDITION

THE REISSUANCE OF *Structural Functions of Harmony* some fifteen years after its first publication is an important event for a number of reasons: not only does it permit the correction of numerous errors and the inclusion of a much-needed index for accessibility of material, but, more importantly, it offers again the definitive statement of a central musical problem by one of the great creative minds of our time. Appropriately this new edition arrives at a time—eighteen years after its author's death—when Schoenberg's towering influence and authority as composer and theorist have become widely accepted. In fact, his words have greater pertinence today, and for a wider public, than they ever had during his lifetime.

*Structural Functions* can be studied not only as a practical guide in harmonic technique and analysis but, at the same time, as a document of the evolution of Schoenberg's own musical philosophy. In the course of this work one can trace the basic presentation of harmonic principles, their enlargement into a unified system of *monotonality* which, in turn, is applied to the examination of various kinds of musical forms from the eighteenth century to the twentieth, leading, logically and inevitably, to a consideration of their relevance to twelve-tone composition. Schoenberg's statement in the last chapter ("Apollonian Evaluation of a Dionysian Epoch"):

> *One day there will be a theory which abstracts rules from these [twelve-tone] compositions. Certainly, the structural evaluation of these sounds will again be based on their functional potentialities.*

not only has a prophetic ring in our contemporary theory and practice, but also emphasizes his evolutionary concept of musical composition.[1]

As has been noted elsewhere, this work is the result of Schoenberg's teaching in an American university. It includes material collected by his students in class, much of which he improvised on the spot. Discovering then (1936–43) that his

[1] Although Schoenberg himself originally wanted to have this last chapter appear first and was overruled by the first publisher to whom he submitted the manuscript, the present order does not materially alter the inherent consequences leading from the study of harmony to its ultimate goal.

ix

students were poorly prepared, he compiled a number of basic texts in harmony, counterpoint, and composition in an attempt to correct their deficiency.[2] These texts, therefore, strongly emphasize training in fundamentals and can be used by beginners in musical theory; but they also pose new concepts and interpretations which challenge musicians at any stage of their development.

*Structural Functions* stands in direct lineal descent from Schoenberg's first great text, his *Harmonielehre*.[3] Acquaintance with this earlier book is of inestimable value for a thorough understanding of the later text, although Schoenberg, realizing that a complete translation of *Harmonielehre* was not available, undertook a condensation of some of its basic principles in Chapter II of the present work. Among these principles the most important is the concept of *root progressions*. This is the foundation of Schoenberg's explanation of all harmony progressions, involving altered chords as well as simple triads. Starting with this basic assumption, it is applied at first to diatonic harmony, then to chords constructed with substitute tones (Chapter III), to transformations (Chapter V), and finally to vagrant harmonies (Chapter VI). It is recommended that one studies alterations of chords in this order before proceeding to the study of regions. The regions in minor, particularly (see Chapter IV), involve the use of altered chords before their elaboration in succeeding chapters. The other main derivation of altered chords, that of tonic minor and subdominant minor, which plays an important part in the *Harmonielehre,* is now incorporated into the discussion of "Interchangeability of Major and Minor" (Chapter VII).

It is this very change of interpretation, from chord derivation to *region,* which distinguishes *Structural Functions* from the *Harmonielehre* and is its main point of departure. What appeared as modulation in the *Harmonielehre* (and in most other treatises on harmony as well) now becomes part of a unified concept of monotonality (see p. 19 for a complete ex-

---

[2] Besides *Structural Functions of Harmony* these works include *Models for Beginners in Composition* (G. Schirmer, 1942), *Preliminary Exercises in Counterpoint* (Faber and Faber, 1963), and *Fundamentals of Musical Composition* (Faber and Faber, 1967).

[3] Originally published in 1911, subsequently revised in 1922 and reprinted in 1966 (Universal Edition, Vienna), it has been partially translated into English under the title, *Theory of Harmony* (Philosophical Library, New York, 1948).

planation), so that instead of measuring distances from key to key (by their relationship within the circle of fifths) a single tonality (tonic) is accepted as the center of all harmonic movement to and from its various regions. Although Schoenberg had for many years employed terms associated with regions, he did not apply them consistently until his *Models for Beginners in Composition* in 1942: in its Glossary there is a definition of regions which is essentially the one found in *Structural Functions*. However, it is only in the latter work that Schoenberg provides a thorough explanation of their relationships, principally in the "Chart of the Regions" (pp. 20 and 30) and in "Classification of Relationship" (Chapter IX). Admittedly, the theory is not complete; Schoenberg, as was his usual custom, postulated certain hypotheses regarding the main problem of key relationships within a composition — how, in fact, harmony functions in determining the structure of a piece. Of the relationships between the regions many, but not all, are explored, at first in four-part harmony. Moreover, when the regions are later applied to the analysis of examples from literature, many instances occur where other explanations of regions could be given. An examination of the classification of regions (Chapter IX) shows the difficulty of finding simple analyses for indirect and remote relationships. This results from a number of causes — the effect of enharmonic changes, the approach to regions from "flats or sharps," the interchangeability of major and minor, etc. — so that more than one region at a time may be valid. Further ambiguities may be brought about by the multiple meanings of transformations, vagrant harmonies, and other altered chords. It is suggested that theorists and students search for other solutions to these problems of regions.

In cases where the relationships move very rapidly, as in the *Durchführung* [Development section] or among the so-called "free forms" (see Chapter XI), only the concept of *roving harmony* is applicable (see p. 164). Although he seemingly avoids the issue of regions, Schoenberg does not claim that this theory will explain every relationship (see his statement on p. xii). Instead, as he had done in his other theoretical writings, he advances certain concepts which can be absorbed by anyone who is able to master the basic ideas of musical relationships and is not merely satisfied with superficial definitions or attracted by the ephemeral qualities of music. It may be true, as some critics claim, that Schoenberg is essentially a preserver of traditional values rather than the revolutionary he is popularly supposed to be. Unlike most preservers of the past, however, who only seek, by historical or stylistic references, to codify theory within a closed system, his concepts, though rooted in tradition, are vital to our time because they derive from the resources of an ever-enquiring and constantly growing musical intellect. Thus, above all, *Structural Functions* should be approached as a challenge to the musician who wishes to deepen and enrich the understanding and practice of his craft.

LEONARD STEIN

*Los Angeles, California, 1969*

## EDITOR'S PREFACE TO
## THE FIRST EDITION

WRITTEN in the last years of Schoenberg's life, *Structural Functions of Harmony* represents the master's final thoughts on " traditional " harmony, and sums up all his conclusions on the subject subsequent to the *Harmonielehre*. There is no need for me to stress the value and importance of this work; the reader will be able to appreciate this for himself. Having been entrusted by Mrs. Schoenberg with the task of preparing the book for publication, I need only explain the extent of such " editing " as has been done. This has mainly consisted of purely grammatical alterations designed to make easier reading here and there, without altering Schoenberg's thought in any way. In addition some explanatory phrases have been interpolated; these are enclosed in square brackets. Schoenberg's prose style was always extremely compressed, even elliptical; and these interpolations are merely designed to bring out the meaning more easily.

The remaining problem is that of the technical terms used. Many of these were devised by Schoenberg himself, and do not correspond to the normal American or English usages; as Mrs. Schoenberg says: " He was striving sometimes for days to find the right expression if he felt that many of the usual terms were misleading and erroneous and did not correspond to the meaning ". In these circumstances, and also in view of the fact that the book is designed for both American and English readers, whose musical nomenclature often varies considerably from each other's, clearly the right course is to leave Schoenberg's musical terms without alteration, and to provide an explanatory glossary of those terms which differ from either American or English usage. This will be found on p. 197.

In conclusion, I would draw the reader's special attention to the Chart of the Regions (p. 20); thorough mastery of the symbols contained in this chart is essential for the understanding of the analyses in the latter part of the book. In particular, it is important to remember Schoenberg's practice, following the normal German usage, of writing the names of major keys in capitals and of minor keys in small letters, without any explanatory " major " or " minor "—thus **F**= F major; **f**=F minor; **SD**=subdominant major; **sd**= subdominant minor.

My grateful thanks are due to Mr. Leonard Stein of Los Angeles, who helped Schoenberg in the preparation of the book, particularly with regard to the musical examples. His practical assistance and advice have been invaluable.

Many thanks are also due to the following publishers for permission to print quotations from copyright works.

| | |
|---|---|
| Strauss.  Salome | Boosey & Hawkes Ltd. |
| Grieg.  Cello Sonata<br>Reger.  Violin Concerto | Hinrichsen Edition Ltd., the proprietors of Peters Edition. |
| Schoenberg.  Der Wanderer<br>            Lockung<br>            1st Chamber Symphony<br>            Pelleas & Melisande | By arrangement with Universal Edition (Alfred A. Kalmus, London) |
| Dvorak.  New World Symphony | Alfred Lengnick & Co., Ltd. |
| Debussy.  Images | Edition Jean Jobert and United Music Publishers Limited |

HUMPHREY SEARLE

*London*

# THE USE OF THIS BOOK FOR TEACHING
## AND SELF-INSTRUCTION

THIS book contains in condensed form the methods of teaching harmony as presented in my *Harmonielehre*. Those whose training is based on these methods will easily be able to follow the more remote conclusions on the evaluation of structural functions. Unfortunately the understanding of harmony by many students is superficial, and foreign to the procedures of great composers. This is caused by the general use of two obsolete teaching methods. One, consisting of writing parts above a figured bass, is much too easy a task; the other, harmonizing a given melody, is too difficult. Both are basically wrong.

Practising part-writing is the only achievement of the figured-bass method. The expectation that becoming familiar with correct harmonic progressions will train the ear is not justified. If such were the case, familiarity with good music would make further teaching superfluous. Besides, playing from figured bass is no longer customary. I suppose that my generation was the last to know it. Today even good organists prefer written-out harmonies to the obsolete shorthand notation.

Harmonizing given melodies is in contradiction to the process of composition; a composer invents melody and harmony simultaneously. Subsequent correction may sometimes be necessary; improvements anticipating later developments and adaptations for changed purposes may challenge the composer's technique. One might also be obliged to harmonize a melody—a folksong, or one by a " one-finger composer ". Again, this can be done only by one who has been born with or has acquired the sense for the evaluation of harmony.

More than forty years of experience have proved to me that it is not difficult to study harmony according to the method of my *Harmonielehre*—that is, to compose harmony progressions from the very beginning. It is also the intention of this book to provide students who have been taught in other ways with a full insight into this technique. Basic advice for this purpose is given in Chapter II; additional recommendations appear in the following chapters.

Of course, part-leading must not be allowed to be a handicap to one who attempts these advanced studies. One who cannot control four parts with a certain ability either has not worked seriously or is entirely untalented and should give up music at once.

Knowing the *treatment of dissonances*, obeying the advice for the use of root progressions, and understanding the process of " neutralization "[1] will provide the background for further conclusions. It is important to relate " substitutes "[2] and " transformations "[3] to degrees[4], and to understand that they do not alter the structural functions of the progressions. They intensify the affinity between tones and promote melodically convincing part-leading.

It should not be overlooked that harmonies with multiple meaning—the " vagrants "[5]—may occasionally proceed in conflict with the theory of root progressions. This is one of the short-comings of every theory—and this theory cannot claim to be an exception; no theory can exclude everything that is wrong, poor, or even detestable, or include everything that is right, good, or beautiful.

The best I can aim at is to recommend such procedures as will seldom be wrong, to draw the attention of the student to the fact that there are distinctions to be made, and to give some advice as to how the evaluation of harmonic progressions will help him to recognize his own shortcomings.

[1] See p. 18 and p. 24.

[2] cf. Chapter III.

[3] cf. Chapter V.

[4] "Degree" means the *root* and the *chord* constructed on a degree of the scale. " The tones of the scale, each of which is the root or lowest tone of a triad, are called *degrees* " (Schoenberg, *Harmonielehre*, p. 35; *Theory of Harmony*, p. 11.)

[5] See Chapter VI.

# STRUCTURAL FUNCTIONS
## OF HARMONY

## PUBLISHER'S NOTE

CERTAIN CORRECTIONS that could not be accommodated in the body of the text have been placed in an Appendix (p. 198). An asterisk in the margin of the text indicates that additional material will be found in the Appendix.

# CHAPTER I

## STRUCTURAL FUNCTIONS OF HARMONY

A TRIAD standing alone is entirely indefinite in its harmonic meaning; it may be the tonic of one tonality or one degree of several others. The addition of one or more other triads can restrict its meaning to a lesser number of tonalities. A certain order promotes such a *succession* of chords to the function of a *progression*.

A *succession* is aimless; a *progression* aims for a definite goal. Whether such a goal may be reached depends on the continuation. It might promote this aim; it might counteract it.

A *progression* has the function of establishing or contradicting a tonality. The combination of harmonies of which a progression consists depends on its purpose—whether it is establishment, modulation, transition, contrast, or reaffirmation.

A *succession* of chords may be *functionless*, neither expressing an unmistakable tonality nor requiring a definite continuation. Such successions are frequently used in descriptive music (see Ex. 1).

The harmony of popular music often consists only of a *mere interchange* of tonic and dominant (Ex. 2), in higher forms concluded by a cadence. Though a mere interchange is primitive, it still has the function of expressing a tonality. Ex. 3 illustrates beginnings with mere interchange of I—IV, I—II, and even I—IV of the submediant region.[1]

\* See CHART OF THE REGIONS, p. 20

The centripetal function of progressions is exerted by stopping centrifugal tendencies, i.e., by establishing a tonality through the conquest of its contradictory elements.

*Modulation* promotes centrifugal tendencies by loosening the bonds of affirmative elements.[2] If a modulation leads to

[1] For the *regions*, see Chapter III.
[2] i.e. Elements which affirm one definite tonality.]

another region or tonality, cadential progressions may establish this region. This occurs in subsections, preliminary endings, contrasting additions of subordinate themes, connecting passages with the purpose of co-ordination and subordination, transitions, and in modulatory sections of scherzos, sonatas, symphonies, etc.

*Roving* harmony is often to be observed in modulatory sections—for example, in fantasies, recitatives, etc.[1] The difference between a modulation and roving harmony is illustrated in Ex. 4. Evidently in Ex. 4b, c, d, no succession of three chords can unmistakably express a region or a tonality.

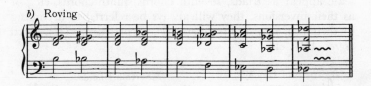

---

[1] See The So-called "Free Forms", p. 165 f.

# CHAPTER II

## PRINCIPLES OF HARMONY
### (A Brief Recapitulation)

HARMONY teaches:

Firstly, the constitution of chords, that is, which tones and how many of them can be sounded simultaneously in order to produce consonances and the traditional dissonances: triads, seventh chords, ninth chords, etc., and their inversions.

Secondly, the manner in which chords should be used in succession: to accompany melodies and themes; to control the relation between main and subordinate voices; to establish a tonality at the beginning and at the end (cadence); or, on the other hand, to abandon a tonality (modulation and remodulation).

Whether the chords built on the seven tones of the major scale appear as triads, seventh chords, ninth chords, etc., or as their inversions, they will always be referred to according to their *root*, i.e., as first *degree* (I), second *degree* (II), third *degree* (III), etc.

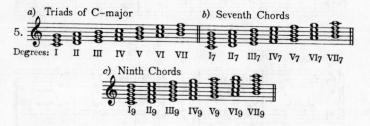

*a)* Triads of C-major      *b)* Seventh Chords

5.

Degrees: I   II   III   IV   V   VI   VII     $I_7$   $II_7$   $III_7$   $IV_7$   $V_7$   $VI_7$   $VII_7$

*c)* Ninth Chords

$I_9$   $II_9$   $III_9$   $IV_9$   $V_9$   $VI_9$   $VII_9$

## PART LEADING

When connecting chords it is advisable that each of the four voices (soprano, alto, tenor and bass, generally used to present harmonic successions) should move no more than necessary.[1] Accordingly large leaps are avoided, and if two chords have a tone in common it should, if possible, be held over in the same voice.

---

[1] " Sie gehorchen dem *Gesetz* des nächsten Weges " (They obey the *law* of the shortest way), Anton Bruckner taught his class at the Vienna University.

This advice is sufficient to avoid the greatest mistakes in part leading, though special precautions are necessary to avoid open or hidden parallel octaves or fifths. Contrary rather than parallel motion is recommended.

### DISSONANCES AND THEIR TREATMENT

While consonances such as simple triads, if faulty parallels are avoided, can be connected unrestrictedly, dissonances require special treatment. In a seventh chord the dissonance usually descends one step to become the third or fifth of the following harmony, or is held over to become its octave.

Treatment of Dissonances

If ninth chords are used, a similar treatment of both seventh and ninth is necessary.

### OUTER VOICES

Of greatest importance is the construction of the two outer voices, soprano and bass. Leaps and successions of leaps which tradition calls unmelodic should be avoided; both voices need not become melodies, but should possess as much variety as possible without violating the rules of part-leading. In the bass, which one might rightfully call the " second melody ", 6-chords, $\frac{6}{4}$-chords, $\frac{6}{5}$-chords, $\frac{4}{3}$-chords and 2-chords should frequently be used in place of root positions of triads and seventh chords. But the $\frac{6}{4}$-chord, when not a mere passing harmony, should be reserved for the " $\frac{6}{4}$-chord of the cadence ".

Remember: in a 2-chord the dissonance is in the bass, and must accordingly descend to a $\frac{6}{3}$-chord.

## ROOT PROGRESSIONS

Note: there is a difference between the bass of a chord and its root. In a 6-chord the third is in the bass; in a $\frac{4}{3}$-chord the fifth is in the bass, etc.

The structural meaning of a harmony depends exclusively upon the degree of the scale. The appearance of the third, fifth or seventh in the bass serves only for greater variety in the " second melody ". Structural functions are exerted by *root progressions*.

There are three kinds of root progressions:

(1) *Strong* or *ascending* progressions:[1]

    (a) A fourth up, identical with a fifth down:

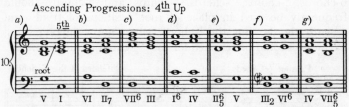

[1] The term *strong* is used because great changes in the constitution of the chord are produced. When the root progresses a fourth up the root note of the first chord is degraded, becoming only the fifth of the second chord. In the case of the root progression a third down, the root note of the first chord is degraded even further, becoming the third of the second chord. The term *ascending* is used in order to avoid the term *weak* progressions in contrast to *strong*. *Weak* qualities have no place in an artistic structure. This is why the second category of root progressions is not called *weak* but *descending*. For more on this subject see Arnold Schoenberg: *Harmonielehre.* p. 140. *Theory of Harmony*, p. 69 ff.

## (b) A third down:

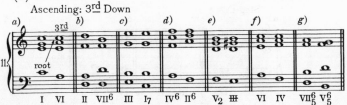

## (2) *Descending* progressions:[1]

### (a) A fourth down:

## (b) A third up:

## (3) *Superstrong* progressions:[2]

### (a) One step up:

[1] They do not possess the conquering power of the *ascending* progressions. On the contrary, they promote the advancement of inferior tones. In I–V, II–VI, III–VII, etc., the fifth of the first chord always advances to become the root of the second. And in I–III, II–IV, III–V, etc., a tone of inferior importance, the third, advances to become the root.

[2] In both cases all the tones of the first chord are " conquered ", i.e. eliminated entirely.

(b) One step down:

"Ascending" progressions can be used without restriction, but the danger of monotony, as, for example, in the circle of consecutive fifths, must be kept under control.

"Descending" progressions, while sometimes appearing as a mere interchange (I–V–V–I, I–IV–IV–I), are better used in combinations of three chords which, like **I**–V–**VI** or **I**–III–**VI**, result in a strong progression (see especially Ex. 17 e).

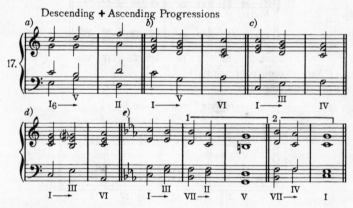

Superstrong progressions often appear as *deceptive*[1] [i.e. false] progressions, generally when the first chord is a dominant (or an "artificial dominant," etc.; see Chapter III), in the

---

[1] The term "deceptive cadence" should be replaced by deceptive *progression*, since there is no cadence: the superstrong progression avoids a cadence.

progressions V–VI, V–IV (~~III~~–IV, ~~III~~–II).[1] Traditionally, in the progression V–IV, IV appears as a 6-chord, and the progression V–VI is seldom used otherwise than from one root position to another.

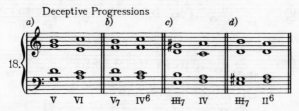

Superstrong progressions may be considered too strong for continuous use.

### THE MINOR TONALITY

Our two main tonalities, major and minor, derive historically from the church modes. The contents of the three major-like modes—Ionian, Lydian and Mixolydian—are concentrated in the one major tonality, and the contents of the three minor-like modes—Dorian, Phrygian and Aeolian—in the same manner, are concentrated in the minor.

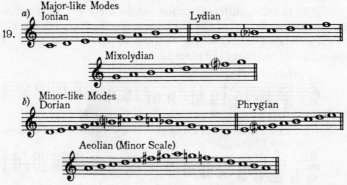

Because of this origin, the minor tonality consists of two scale forms. The tones of the descending form do not differ from those of the relative major scale. The ascending form substitutes for its natural seventh tone a leading tone a half-step higher. Often, to lead more smoothly to the substitute

---

[1] Crossed Roman numerals—~~VI~~, ~~V~~, ~~III~~, ~~II~~, etc., indicate that the chords are altered through the use of substitute tones.

seventh tone, the natural sixth tone is also replaced by a tone a half-step higher.[1]

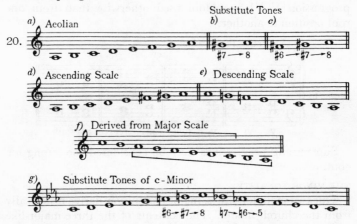

Ascending and descending scale forms (sixth and seventh tones) should not be intermixed, but kept apart to avoid cross-relations.

The inclusion of substitute tones in the minor tonality produces thirteen different triads, while there are only seven in the major. When advice has been given for " *neutralization* " of cross-related tones, it will become apparent that some of these chords endanger the tonality.[2]

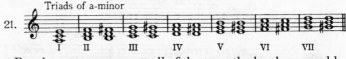

For the same reason not all of the seventh chords are usable.

The treatment of *dissonances* in the minor is often obstructed by the necessity of keeping a substitute tone apart from its natural tone. The discrepancy between the *treatment of the*

---

[1] J. S. Bach frequently uses the substitute seventh and sixth tones when descending for melodic reasons.

[2] For more about the process of *neutralization* see p. 18 and Arnold Schoenberg: *Hamonielehre*, p. 116. *Theory of Harmony*, p. 49.

*dissonance* (i.e. its necessity either to be held over or to fall) and the necessity of the leading tone to rise is the cause of some problems.

Augmented and diminished steps are traditionally considered unmelodic.

In Ex. 23 a number of progressions are illustrated.

*a)* Ascending Progressions

23.

| I | IV | I | VI | I | VI₇ | II⁶ | V | II | V |

III⁶ VI    III   VI    III   I    III   I    etc.

*b)* Descending Progressions

I ⟶ V ⟶ IV⁶    I ⟶ V ⟶ VI    I ⟶ III ⟶ VI

*c)* Superstrong Progressions

V   VI    III   IV⁶    III⁶   IV⁶    etc.

ESTABLISHMENT OF TONALITY

THE CADENCE I

A tonality is expressed by the exclusive use of all its tones. A scale (or part of one) and a certain order of the harmonies affirm it more definitely. In classical and popular music, a mere interchange of I and V is sufficient if not contradicted by extra-tonal harmonies. In most cases, for sharper

definition, a *cadence* is added at the end of an entire piece
or of its sections, segments, and even smaller units.

Distinguishing a tonality from those tonalities which
resemble it most is the first step towards its unmistakable
establishment. **C** major differs from **G** major (Dominant) and
**F** major (Subdominant) by only one tone in each case, **f♯** and
**b♭** respectively. But it also has many tones and triads in common with **a** minor (submediant), **e** minor (mediant), and
even **d** minor (dorian). Thus, Ex. 24a illustrates that the
first three triads admit the establishment of **C** major as well
as **G** major or **e** minor. Similarly, in 24b such "neutral" triads
can be in **C** major, **a** minor or **F** major; and three neutrals
in 24c can be continued in **C** major or **d** minor. A succession
of neutral triads fail to establish a tonality.

[In the following examples the various tonalities—from **C**
major—are expressed in terms of regions: **T**, **D**, **m**, **sm**, **SD**,
and **dor**. See CHART OF THE REGIONS, p. 20.]

The chords which express a tonality unmistakably are the three main triads: I, IV and V. IV, by contradicting the **f♯**, excludes the dominant of **G** major; the **b♮** of V excludes the subdominant's **b♭**. In the cadence the traditional order is IV–V–I, consisting of the superstrong progression IV–V and the ascending V–I.

V in the cadence is never replaced by another degree and appears exclusively in root position. But IV is often replaced by II (ascending to V) or by VI (superstrong to V).

### THE $\frac{6}{4}$-CHORD OF THE CADENCE

The $\frac{6}{4}$-chord of the cadence is often considered as a prepared or unprepared dissonance to be resolved into V (see Ex. 27 a, b). By convention this function of the $\frac{6}{4}$-chord has acquired such prominence that it is often misleading if a $\frac{6}{4}$-chord, especially on a degree other than I, appears in another context (see Ex. 27 c, d).

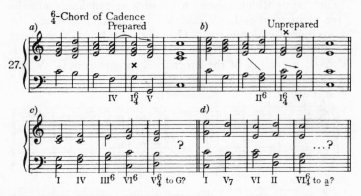

### THE HALF CADENCE: OTHER CADENCES

Half cadences bring forth all degrees belonging to a full cadence, but, instead of proceeding to I, stop on V: e.g. IV–V, II–V or VI–V.

Plagal cadences, IV–I or II–I, and the phrygian cadence, II–III (or ~~III~~), are only a means of stylistic expression and are structurally of no importance.

# CHAPTER III

## SUBSTITUTES AND REGIONS

### DERIVATION OF THE SUBSTITUTES[1]

Just as the substitute tones in the minor scale are derived from the Aeolian mode, several other substitutes are derived from the remaining modes. They may belong to an ascending scale—like the artificial leading (seventh) tones of Dorian, Mixolydian, Aeolian and occasionally also Phrygian—or to a descending scale—like the minor sixth in Dorian and the perfect fourth in Lydian.

[1 i.e. "Borrowed" tones or notes.]

In Ex. 29 the modes and their substitutes are shown in reference to a C major scale, and in transpositions to B♭ and A major, and are classified as ascending or descending substitutes. By substituting for [altering] the third in minor triads, they produce "artificial" major triads and "artificial" dominant seventh chords (Ex. 30 a, b). Substituting for [altering] the fifth changes minor triads to "artificial" diminished triads (30c), commonly used with an added seventh as in (30f), and changes major triads to augmented (30d). Note also the diminished seventh chords[1] (30e) and the artificial minor triad on V.[2](30g).

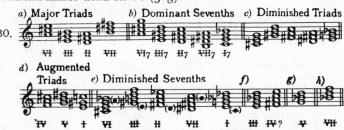

Artificial dominants, artificial dominant seventh chords, and artificial diminished seventh chords are normally used in progressions according to the models V–I, V–VI and V–IV, i.e. the authentic leap a fourth up and the two superstrong progressions, a second up and down. This is because their thirds are leading tones.

[1] The seventh of a diminished seventh chord will be treated here as the ninth of a ninth chord whose root is omitted (see Chapter V, Transformations).

[2] A dominant is a major triad. If a minor third replaces the natural third this triad must be called *five-minor* (v). [i.e. $\frac{3}{5}$♭].

Artificial Dominants (V–I, V–VI, V–IV)

Diminished Sevenths

The artificial minor chord on V preferably follows the model of IV—V in minor. But V̶–I̶ (Ex. 32c) or V̶–IV (32d) will also be found.

Diminished triads, in the 19th century, appear more frequently with the added minor seventh. The same is true of the artificial diminished triads on III, which forms successions resembling II–V, II–I and II–III of minor.

The artificial dominant on II is the first of the *transformations* of this degree (see Chapter V) which are much in use, especially in cadences, where they introduce either $I_4^6$ or $V_7$.

## INTRODUCTION OF SUBSTITUTES

Tones foreign to the scale can be introduced either quasi-diatonically or chromatically. Both procedures are melodic improvements of the part-leading and seldom involve a change of the degree.

Quasi-diatonic introduction is best carried out in a way similar to the introduction of the seventh and sixth tones in the minor. The substitute seventh tone is a leading tone and must ascend to the eighth tone [octave]. A substitute sixth tone should not lead to a natural sixth or seventh tone, nor should a natural sixth or seventh tone be followed by a substitute sixth or seventh tone. Substitute tones are "neutralized" by ascending, natural tones by descending (35c). However, the natural sixth tone is combined with the substitute seventh in a diminished seventh chord (36e).

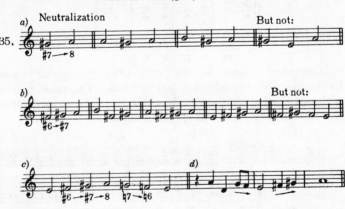

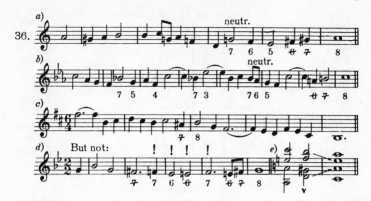

## REGIONS I

Only four ascending and one descending leading tones were used in the modes (cf. p.15). These and other substitutes are derived from the relation of a tonality to segments of it which are carried out like independent tonalities: the *regions*. This consideration serves to provide a more profound understanding of the unity in the harmony of a piece.

Intermixing of substitute tones and chords with otherwise diatonic progressions, even in non-cadential segments, was considered by former theorists as modulation. This is a narrow and, therefore, obsolete concept of tonality. One should not speak of modulation unless a tonality has been abandoned definitely and for a considerable time, and another tonality has been established harmonically as well as thematically.

The concept of regions is a logical consequence of the principle of *monotonality*. According to this principle, every digression from the tonic is considered to be still within the tonality, whether directly or indirectly, closely or remotely related. In other words, there is only *one tonality* in a piece, and every segment formerly considered as another tonality is only a region, a harmonic contrast within that tonality.

Monotonality includes modulation—movement towards another *mode* and even establishment of that mode. But it considers these deviations as regions of the tonality, subordinate to the central power of a tonic. Thus comprehension of the harmonic unity within a piece is achieved.

In the following chart the regions are presented by symbols in an order which indicates their relationship.

### CHART OF THE REGIONS

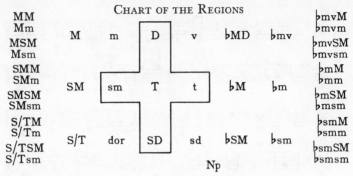

#### ABBREVIATIONS

| | | | | | |
|---|---|---|---|---|---|
| **T** | means | tonic | **Np** | means | Neapolitan |
| **D** | „ | dominant | **dor** | „ | Dorian |
| **SD** | „ | subdominant | **S/T** | „ | supertonic |
| **t** | „ | tonic minor | **♭M** | „ | flat mediant major |
| **sd** | „ | subdominant minor | **♭SM** | „ | flat submediant major |
| **v** | „ | five-minor | **♭MD** | „ | flat mediant major's dominant |
| **sm** | „ | submediant minor | **♭m** | „ | flat mediant minor |
| **m** | „ | mediant minor | **♭sm** | „ | flat submediant minor |
| **SM** | „ | submediant major | **♭mv** | „ | flat mediant minor's five |
| **M** | „ | mediant major | | | |

[*N.B.* All symbols in capitals refer to major keys; those in small letters to minor keys.]

The first symbol always indicates the relation to the tonic. The second symbol shows the relation to the region indicated by the first symbol. Thus: **Mm** reads "mediant major's mediant minor"(in **C,** a minor region on **g♯**); **SMsm** reads "submediant major's submediant minor" (in **C,** a minor region on **f♯**); ♭**smSM** reads "flat submediant minor's submediant major" (in **C** a major region on **F♭**), etc.

The tonics of the regions of **C** major are presented below, corresponding to the relations shown in the preceding chart.

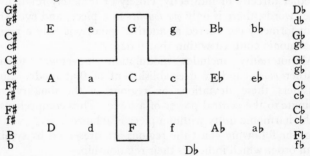

The regions closest related to a tonic are those in the centre of the chart: dominant region (**D**), subdominant region (**SD**), submediant region (**sm**) and tonic minor region (**t**). In Chapter IX the regions are classified as: I. Close and Direct; II. Indirect but Close; III. Indirect; IV. Indirect and Remote; V. Distant.

### INTRODUCTION OF REGIONS

Among the regions which resemble the modes, three are major-like (**T, D, SD**) and three minor-like (**dor, m, sm**). The minor-like regions substitute [alter] those tones which make them similar to relative minor (**sm**).

Similarly, the major-like regions replace natural tones with substitutes, in order to simulate major tonalities.

Modulation from one region to another—after neutralization of cross-related tones has been carried out—is based on *at least one harmony [chord] common to both regions*. Whether a region has to be established by a cadence depends on its compositorial purpose. Substitute tones alone, however, will seldom suffice to establish it distinctly. Three or more of the characteristics of a region should be present. In every other respect the advice given for the quasi-diatonic introduction of substitutes (cf. p. 18) applies here also.

In Ex. 41 substitutes are used without the establishment of a region. Here, they merely produce enrichment by enhancing the part-leading. Ex. 41f, which consists of the same root progressions as 41e, does not use any substitutes, and thus illustrates how effective substitutes are in enriching the harmony. In these examples (at ✕) chromatic progressions are used occasionally, especially in order to facilitate melodic part-leading.

## CHROMATIC PROCEDURE

Chromatic ascent produces upward leading tones; chromatic descent produces downward leading tones.

In **C** major, the ascending leading tones from **f** to **g**, **g** to **a** and **c** to **d** should be written respectively **f♯**, **g♯** and **c♯**, and not **g♭**, **a♭** and **d♭**. Similarly, the descending leading tones should be written **b♭** between **b** and **a**, **e♭** between **e** and **d**, **a♭** between **a** and **g** and **d♭** between **d** and **c**. But between **g** and **f** the notation should preferably be accommodated to the tonality and key signature; the **f♯** of Ex. 43b is preferable to the **g♭** of 43a.

If remote transformations[1] of a seventh chord are used, as in 43c and 43d, **e♯** might be written instead of **f**. But in tonalities with many sharps or flats the notation is often simplified rather illogically, irrespective of the harmonic meaning. In 42b at ✕, the **c♯** in the bass is evidently the third of IV of **m** and it would be senseless to spoil the recognizability of the chord by pedantically writing **d♭**. It is advisable not to contradict the key-signature, and in more remote regions chromatic substitutes should be written as if the key-signature were changed. Note the changing notation of the same pitch at ✛ (Ex. 44).

[1] See Chapter V, Transformations.

Chromatic procedure, if it does not alter the harmonic progression, is, like substitution, a purely melodic matter arising out of the part-leading. It is useless if it does not render the progressions smooth.

In Ex. 46 chromatic procedures, though in the form of *enriched cadences*, express nothing else than the tonic region.

In Ex. 47 introduction of various regions and modulation back to the tonic is illustrated.

Alternatives to 47b (see p.29)
Half Cadences

Full Cadences

In Ex. 47a, IV of **T** is identical with VI of **sm**; accordingly V of **sm** (at ✕) can follow, as the **g** of the beginning has been neutralized. After this the harmonies are *registered*[1] in **sm**, until I of **sm** (at ∠) is considered as VI of **T**. The return to **T** is then carried out through **II**. The cadence in this case is rather rich because of the long extension of **sm**; it uses successively **III**7, **VI**2, II and **II**.

In 47b the problem of moving from **SD** to **D** is carried out indirectly in order to introduce one harmony common to both; III of **SD**=II of **D** (at ✕).

**Dor** to **m**, as in 47i, is a longer way than one might suspect because there are not many characteristic harmonies in common. The same is true of all regions whose tonics are only one step apart: **SD** to **D**, **D** to **sm**, etc. (See Remotely Related Intermediate Regions, p. 65f.).

Those harmonies in which one or more natural or substitute tones can be employed as ascending or descending leading tones are considered most characteristic. For this reason, in 47i, I of **T** must at once be considered as VII of **dor**.

Examples which end in the tonality with which they began can be considered as *enriched cadences*, even if several regions

---

[1 i.e. The music is considered as being temporarily in that region.]

have been passed through. Examples which do not return to the tonality of the beginning are *modulations*.

### FUNCTIONAL LIMITATIONS OF ARTIFICIAL DOMINANTS

A dominant with the function of V–I must be a major triad whose third is either natural or introduced quasi-diatonically (cf. p. 18). Accordingly the quasi-diatonically introduced artificial dominants on II, III, VI and VII ("substituting" a major third and, in the case of VII, a perfect fifth also), and on I (adding a minor seventh) can function like V–I (or V–VI) within their regions (at x in Ex. 48a). In contrast to this, an artificial dominant whose major third is chromatically introduced is functionally not a dominant, and the degree a fourth above it is not the tonic of any region (at x in Ex. 48b).

In every other respect artificial dominants, provided their "substitute" tones follow their natural tendency, can progress as if no alteration had occurred, i.e. according to the models V–I, V–VI, V–IV. Other progressions may appear in free composition in order to express some formal or emotional purpose; thus, one may find in masterworks a chromatically produced V leading to a final I as if the former were a real dominant. But such deviations cannot be tolerated in bare harmonic examples.

THE CADENCE II (ENRICHED)

Ex. 46b, 46d and 47c, d, e are alternative endings producing
half cadences to V of **T**, V of **sm**, V of **m** and V of **dor**. They
contain many substitute harmonies. In Ex. 47f, g and h, full
cadences to the same regions are carried out, i.e. to I of **sm,**
I of **m** and I of **dor**. In some cases *transformations* have been
used (marked + in Exs. 46–48) which will be discussed later
(p. 35).

# CHAPTER IV

## REGIONS IN MINOR

### REGIONS II

In establishing the relationships among the regions in minor,[1] it must be kept in mind that the minor tonality is a residue of one of the modes, the Aeolian. As such, it uses the seven tones of the diatonic (Ionian) scale, and produces all its characteristic differences by means of substitutes. As a mere stylistic convention, it had acquired the emotional quality of sadness in the vocabulary of the classical composers, in spite of the many gay folk-songs in minor-like modes.

From the standpoint of structural functions, a minor tonic does not maintain as direct a control over its regions as a major tonic. Thus the number of directly related regions is small, and modulation to indirectly related regions through its relative major (**M**), tonic major (**T**), dominant (**D**), etc., is definitely more remote.

### CHART OF THE REGIONS IN MINOR[2]

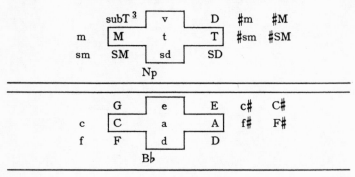

While a major tonality, i.e. the tonic, has at least the power of a dominant over its subdominant, such a power is denied to the tonic of a minor tonality; a dominant must be a major triad (see p. 16).

[1] See Classification of Regions in Minor, p. 75.

[2] See abbreviations, p. 20.

[3] The term " supertonic " (**S/T**) indicates that the root of this region lies two fifths *above* the tonic. Correspondingly, the term " subtonic " (**subT**) is introduced here, indicating that the root of this region lies two fifths *below* the tonic of a minor tonality.

The order of the regions in the chart of minor is the reverse of the order in major (see p. 20). In spite of the close relations, the change of *gender* (i.e. from minor to major keys) requires caution and careful neutralization.

Again the regions in the centre of the chart must be considered as the closest related. Nevertheless in masterworks the first part of binary or ternary forms will just as often end on dominant (**D**) as on **v** [a minor triad on the fifth degree], especially if a repetition is demanded to whose tonic a dominant leads more powerfully. Obviously the regions on the right side of the chart are even more distantly related than those in major on the same side.

The examples, 49 a—e, demonstrate passing through the following regions: **M, v, sd, D, SM** and **T**.

In Ex. 49a I of **v** is avoided through the deceptive progression to VI of **v** (at ×, ms. 4), thus facilitating the turn to **M**. " Registration " of harmonies in two or more regions (cf. p. 27) explains their relationship. In 49b the diminished 7th chord (× in ms. 2) is repeated in a different notation in ms. 3 with a different meaning, a procedure very often used in this and following examples, not only for instructional but also for structural purposes; the multiple use of such harmonies has a smoother effect.

In 49d the diminished 7th chord in ms. 5 (×) is " registered " in three regions; this is not uncommon for a diminished 7th chord.

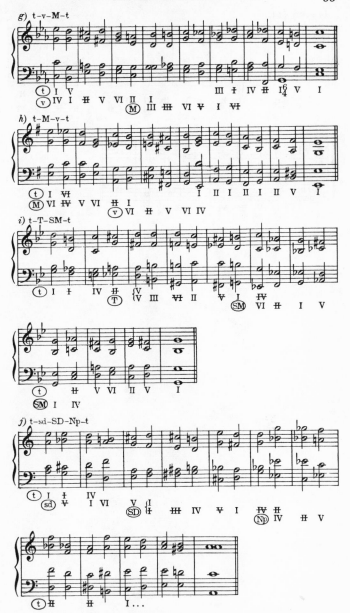

# CHAPTER V

## TRANSFORMATIONS

Richness and greater variety of harmony are based on the relationship between a tonality and its regions, on the substitutions which are produced in the harmonies through the influence of this relationship, and on the possibility of using harmonies in a manner different from their original derivations. Many such chords deserve the name *vagrant* harmonies because they seem to wander nomadically between regions, if not tonalities, without ever settling down. Nevertheless, every "transformation" [altered chord] must be registered as a degree belonging to one of the regions; thus, even seemingly unusual progressions will prove to be normal.

### TRANSFORMATIONS OF THE SECOND DEGREE (II)

"Transformations" of the second degree result from the influence of **D**, **SD** and **sd** (for *subdominant minor* see Chapter VII). Under the influence of **D**, the [minor] third of II is substituted for, as discussed under *Artificial Dominants* (p. 28), by a major third. Substituting for the fifth of II a tone from **sd** or **t** produces a diminished triad. Most of these transformations are employed as seventh and ninth chords.

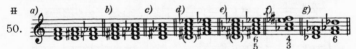

In Ex. 50c both **D** and **sd** are operative. The same is the case in d, e and f, while g, the Neapolitan sixth chord, is borrowed unchanged from **sd** where it is a natural VI. All the forms in d, e and f are basically ninth chords, though in their normal use the root is omitted. Diminished seventh chords, as 50d, were formerly considered seventh chords on natural or artificial leading tones. Accordingly a diminished seventh chord in **c** minor (b–d–f–a♭) would be considered to be on VII and, worse, 50d would be considered as based on a "substituted" root (f♯), an assumption which must be rejected as nonsensical. Besides the progressions VII–I and IV–V then look like *deceptive* progressions, while their function as V–I and II–V is truly *authentic*. Registering every diminished seventh chord as a ninth chord on II (or V, or any other degree), root omitted, prevents it being used as a "Jack-of-all-trades" and enforces consciousness of the structural functions of the root progressions.[1]

Foreign tones can again be introduced either quasi-diatonically or chromatically as in the following examples.

Several forms of these transformations can be used in succession; chromatic progressions are helpful here. Change of notation is sometimes advisable but should not obscure the reference to the degree of the scale.

The tones of the Neapolitan sixth chord appear occasionally in **root** position. It will then be called the *Neapolitan triad* ( at * ).

[1] For more on this subject see Arnold Schoenberg: *Harmonielehre*, p. 234; *Theory of Harmony*, p. 144.

On account of their functional similarity to the dominant and to artificial dominants, transformations appear most frequently in progressions after the models of V–I, V–VI, V–IV; i.e. ⇟–V, ⇟–I, ⇟–III.

I   IV   ♯♯   ♯   ♯♯   ♯♯   I⁶₄   V   I

In 54a (*) observe the progression e♭ to e♮. As e♭ is the ninth of II, it should either descend or be sustained like 54e (*), where it prepares the third of a minor tonic. But if a major tonic follows it is necessary to use a *silent* enharmonic change treating the e♭ as if it were d♯.

In 54b (*) the succession from ♯ (Neapolitan sixth) to III of the tonic minor obscures the tonic major, but might be usable in long examples.

In 54c (at *) a ♯ derived from **sd** is followed by a natural III,—a very harsh progression, because III, as I of the *mediant* region, is very foreign to **sd** (see CHART OF THE REGIONS, p.20).

### TRANSFORMATIONS OF OTHER DEGREES IN THE TONIC REGION

In Ex. 55 the transformations applied to II are now applied to I, III, IV, V, VI, and VII. Some forms are unusable, at first glance. Others which also endanger the tonality might be usable under certain compositional assumptions. Here are examined only the most important progressions, according to the models of V–I, V–VI, and V–IV.

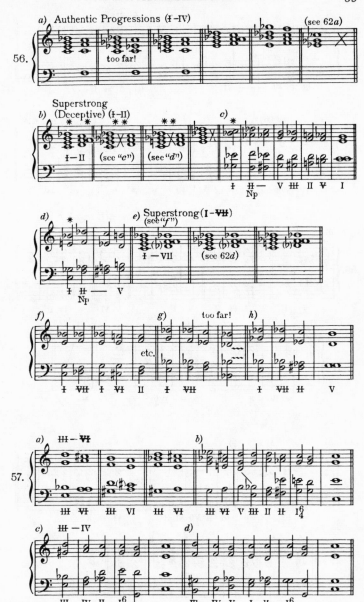

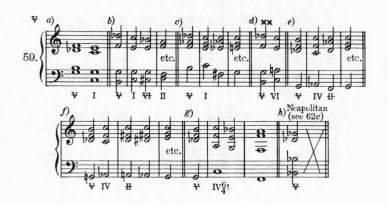

Restrictions (see below)

In order to evaluate the methods of using these transformations, the following restrictions must be followed.

## RESTRICTIONS

Transformation does not change the degree, but some products of it do seem *irreconcilably remote*. The most decisive reason against the introduction of such chords is generally that they are not " borrowed " from closely related regions, as, for instance, the Neapolitan of II. There is no close region containing a **c♭** which justifies a Neapolitan on I like Ex. 55a (at *). The Neapolitans in 55c and d, (at *), on IV and V, may be similarly evaluated.

Because they are so remote, it is also difficult to introduce and resolve the Neapolitans on I, IV and V (Ex. 62a, b, c).

The same applies to all transformations of I, IV and V which substitute a diminished fifth for a perfect fifth, (see Ex. 62d at *). It is, of course, not impossible to reconcile the remoteness of such harmonies by an appropriate continuation, as in 62d, 58a, b, etc. Ex. 56c and d show that the Neapolitan sixth on II can follow, which is entirely acceptable. Traditionally, however, transformations which substitute the diminished fifth for the perfect fifth, tend to be followed by a major triad, according to the model of II–V in minor (62e).

To sum up, the following advice may be given. A succession of two harmonies which appear in remotely and indirectly related regions often produces the effect of intolerable harshness (see Remotely Related Intermediate Regions, p. 65), as, for instance, Ex. 56b ( ∗∗ ) and 59d (× ×). The transformation of I in 56b first appears in the natural triads of the *Neapolitan* region (**D♭**), while the minor triad on **d** might be understood as I of **dor**. The other case (59d) can be similarly judged.

Neapolitan sixths on VI and VII (Ex. 60, 61) lead to $^6_4$-chords of V and VI respectively (or to the dominants on to which they resolve). This can be misleading, on account of the traditional meaning of a $^6_4$-chord. But Ex. 60d, e, f and 61e, f, g, show that it is not too difficult to counteract this tendency.

A I of any region introduced by a transformation of V (Ex. 58b) will not function as a tonic and requires a continuation which will reaffirm it.

In cases like Ex. 57e, an enharmonic change in notation, (**a♭** instead of g♯ at *), disregarding the derivation, is advisable.

Transformations like the preceding can be built on all degrees of all regions. Many of these forms might duplicate forms of less remote regions. Even so the number of cases would be immense. This excludes a thorough evaluation of them; some progressions might be impossible, others might be " dangerous but passable ".

In Ex. 63 transformations in minor are illustrated and one example of their application is added (63h). The principles of their evaluation and the restrictions to be followed do not differ from those of the major key.

Transformations in Minor

63.

# CHAPTER VI

## VAGRANT HARMONIES

MANY of the transformations are vagrant harmonies because of their constitution (diminished sevenths, augmented triads, augmented $^6_5$-chords and $^4_3$-chords, etc.), and also because of their *multiple meaning*.

There exist only three diminished seventh chords and four augmented triads. Accordingly every diminished seventh chord belongs to at least eight tonalities or regions, and every augmented triad belongs, in the same manner, to six tonalities or regions.

By an enharmonic change in their notation, augmented $^6_5$- and $^4_3$-chords can become dominant seventh chords , and vice versa (see Ex. 64c and Ex. 65a at ✕).

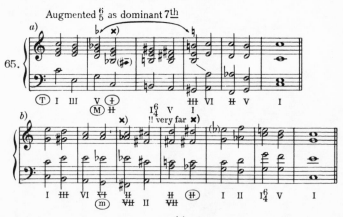

Adding minor sevenths, and minor or major ninths to augmented triads, with or without the root, produces another series of chords which are vagrants by constitution (Ex. 66 and 67; also Ex. 69, marked *L*).

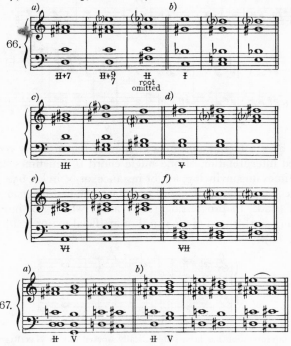

Change of interpretation—whether or not based on the chord constitution—means change of the degree. From the standpoint of structural functions only the *root* of the progression is decisive. But emotional or compositional conditions often require strong contrasts, friction or sudden change.

An example of a surprise modulation can be seen in Ex. 68, from Beethoven's Eighth Symphony. The tone **d♭**, first derived from **sd**, is later interpreted as **c♯**, V of **f♯** minor.

To base a modulation or a change of region solely on the altered interpretation of one single chord is sometimes harsh, sometimes unconvincing, as, for instance, at × in Ex. 65a, b, c.

The Neapolitan sixth chord is, in fact, the first inversion of a major triad. Its progressions, ♯♯–V and ♯♯–I, can be imitated on every sixth chord of a natural or artificial major triad (at x in Ex. 69).

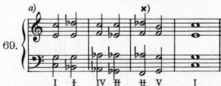

_____
[1] This interpretation has been systematically worked out by Max Reger in a little pamphlet, *Beiträge zur Modulationslehre,* 1903.

be abandoned, while 71b, d and f prove such progressions to be adequate preparations for modulatory movements to **sm, t,** and **m** respectively.

# CHAPTER VII

## INTERCHANGEABILITY OF MAJOR AND MINOR

### (Tonic Minor, Subdominant Minor and v-Minor Regions)

REGIONS III (MAJOR)

A dominant can introduce a major or a minor triad, and can be the dominant of a major or of a minor region. Upon the potency of the dominant is based the interchangeability of major and minor. This power makes the following regions close relatives of a major tonality: tonic minor (**t**), subdominant minor (**sd**), and v-minor (**v**) (cf. p. 56). Because of the principle of interchangeability, the following regions are also closely related: the major forms of mediant (**M**) and submediant (**SM**) and (derived from tonic minor) the major and minor forms of flat mediant (♭**M**, ♭**m**) and flat submediant (♭**SM**, ♭**sm**), which will be discussed as *indirectly related* in the next chapter. Through this relationship numerous substitute chords become available (see Ex. 72).

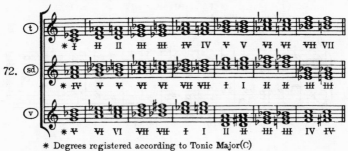

72.

✳ Degrees registered according to Tonic Major(C)

TONIC MINOR REGION

In Ex. 73 substitute harmonies derived from **t** are introduced in various ways. In 73a I of **T** (♭ of **t**) introduces IV of **t**. VI of **t** is followed by a transformation of II of both **I** and **t**. Ex. 73b and c demonstrate that even a longer sojourn in **t** is no obstacle to the re-establishment of **T**. In 73d the deceptive progression V–VI of **t** is followed by a frequent interchange of major and minor. Chromaticism supports the change to **T** in 73e ( at ✕).

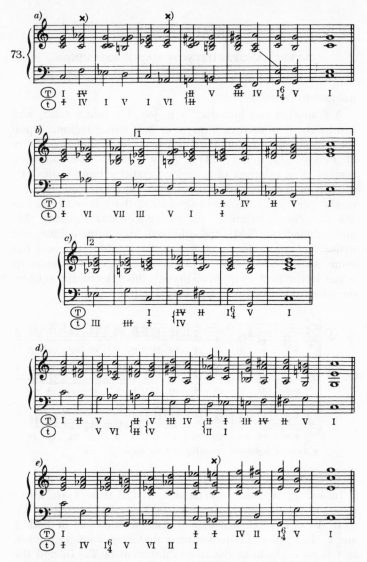

In classical music, major and minor are often exchanged without much ado; a passage in minor follows a passage in major without any harmonic connective, and vice versa.

*a*) Beethoven: Symphony No.2, Larghetto

*b*) Schubert: A minor Quartet, Op.29, 1st Movement (Recapitulation)

SUBDOMINANT MINOR REGION

The successive use of too many harmonies derived from **sd** can obscure the tonality. In mss. 2–3 of 75a not only is the tonality obscured, but **sd** could even be mistaken for ♭**SM** because of an accumulation of harmonies drawn from the descending minor scale. In such a case one might balance the sub-regions [flat keys] by elements of the super-regions, e.g. dorian and mediant, as in this example. Introducing such much more remote regions as ♭**SM** prolongs the examples and requires stronger means to counteract it.

Structurally the Neapolitan sixth is certainly a remote relation of a tonality, though convention has admitted the use of this popular mannerism. But of course the Neapolitan of **sd** (Ex. 75b) is extremely remote. This chord is the cause of all the subsequent shortcomings of 75b. For instance, in ms. 4, iv/iv [i.e. iv of iv] is one of the most remote harmonies. Strong means are required to counterbalance it—vagrant harmonies, diminished seventh chords and chromatic progressions. Unfortunately some of the harmonies cannot be "registered" in two regions; this, at least theoretically, would justify their exclusion [from an example which does not modulate]. The alternative, 75c shows that an early return to **T** is not impossible.

In 75d the change from major to minor is supported by the chromatic progression (ms. 2) in the bass. The Neapolitan sixth, here a natural VI of **sd**, is introduced by an augmented $^6_5$ on ♯. This is enharmonically presented (**g**♭ instead of f♯)

as a 2-chord on III of **sd** (ms. 3).  In the following measure the return to **SD** is prepared through the chromatic step in the tenor, **d♭** to **d♮**.

Alternative to "b"

## FIVE-MINOR REGION (v)

The function of a dominant can only be exerted, as previously stated (p. 16), by a major triad. The term " sub*dominant* " is illogical and " sub*dominant minor* " is wrong. If V dominates I, then I dominates IV, not the reverse. The term " dominant minor " would be mere nonsense; therefore this region will here be called " five-minor " (**v**).[1]

The **v**-region is very well suited to prepare the appearance of **dor** and **SD**. In 76b III of **t** (ms. 4), introduced by a deceptive progression, requires special treatment. In 76c the **v**-region appears through interchange with its major (V).

---

[1] For more on this subject see Arnold Schoenberg: *Harmonielehre*, p. 232; *Theory of Harmony*, p. 139.

# CHAPTER VIII

## INDIRECT BUT CLOSE RELATIONS

(Mediant Major, Submediant Major, Flat Mediant Major
and Minor, Flat Submediant Major and Minor)               *

REGIONS IV

MAJOR

IN BACH'S time all movements of a cyclic work generally
stayed in one tonality, and even the interchange of major and
minor was not too frequent.  In the masterworks of the Classical
and Romantic eras one or both middle movements are to be
found in closely related contrasting tonalities such as **t**, **D**, **SD**,
**sm**, **sd**, **m** and **v**, and also in the more indirectly related
**M**, **SM**, ♭**M**, ♭**SM**.  Most of these relationships, as regions of
Class 1 and 2 (see p. 68), and even of Class 3, appear as
contrasts within a movement.  A few such cases of contrasts
between movements or within a movement illustrate this
point:

**M**: Beethoven Trio Op. 97 in B♭ (3rd movement in D
major); Beethoven Piano Sonata Op. 53 in C (1st movement,
subordinate theme in E major); Brahms 3rd Symphony in F
(1st movement, subordinate theme in A major).

**SM**: Schumann Symphony in E♭ (2nd movement, C major).

♭**M**: Schubert C major Quintet (1st movement, subordinate
theme in E♭ major ).

♭**SM**: Beethoven and Brahms Violin Sonatas in A major
(middle movements in F major); Beethoven Piano Sonata
Op. 7 in E♭ (Largo movement in C major, subordinate theme
in A♭ major).

These masters observed such relationships almost as strictly
as if they were rules.  This proves the validity of the concept
of monotonality.  Nevertheless there exist exceptions—violations
—such as the second movement of Beethoven's C♯ minor
String Quartet, Op. 131, in D major, the F♯ major movement
of Brahms' Second Cello Sonata in F major, etc.

Submediant major (**SM**) and mediant major (**M**) are
related to **sm** and **m** respectively on the basis of the interchangeability of major and minor.  This is an indirect but
very close relation.  Presenting this relation as an equation:

**M:m**  
**SM:sm** $\Big\}$ = **T:t**

The relation of flat submediant (♭**SM**) and flat mediant major (♭**M**) is indirect, based on the relationship of **t** to **T** and **sd** to **SD**:

**t** (c):      ♭**M** (E♭) $\Big\}$ = **sm** (a): **T** (C)  
**sd** (f):     ♭**SM** (A♭)

The movement into these regions applies the inter-change-ability of minor and major to the intermediate regions, thereby taking advantage of common harmonies as before. In **M** and **SM** the introduction of a common dominant will promote the change. A minor chord on IV (i.e. iv) will function as the bridge to ♭**M** and ♭**SM**. Transformations and vagrant harmonies assist in producing smooth transitions.

Interchangeability of major and minor also includes ♭sm, because of ♭**SM**, and ♭**m**, because of ♭**M**.

* **MINOR**

In minor, interchangeability furnishes **m** and **sm**, derived from the descending (natural) scale, and also **♯m** and **♯M**, **♯sm** and **♯SM**, derived from the ascending scale (containing the substitutes).[1] Thus, in an **A**-minor tonality,

    **m**, **sm**, **♯m** and **♯sm** would be minor regions on
    c,   f,    c♯  and f♯;

and

    **♯M** and **♯SM** would be major regions on
    C♯  and F♯.

[1 See also Ex. 49 for **D** and **SM** regions.]

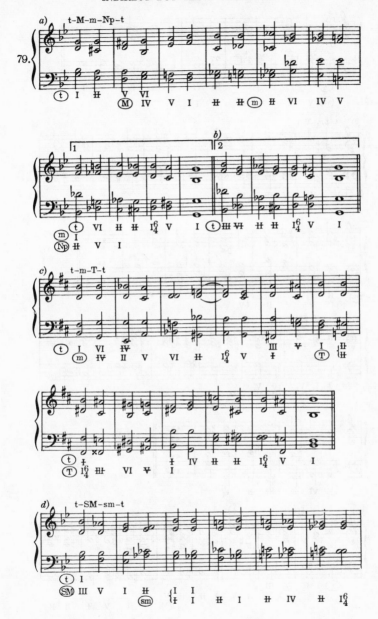

## REMOTELY RELATED INTERMEDIATE REGIONS

The connection of regions which have no common harmonies, such as **v** (in C major, g) and **SM** (A) or ♭**SM** (A♭), **dor** (d) and **M** (E) or ♭**M** (E♭), and **m** (e) or **M** (E) and **SD** (F) or **sd** (f) offers difficulties. Their relation to the main tonality might be indirect but not remote, in spite of which their relation to one another can be as irreconcilably remote as, for instance, that of ♭**M** or ♭**m** with **sm** or **SM**.

The preceding statement may be generalized as follows:

Regions, and even tonalities, whose tonics differ a major or minor second or augmented fourth (diminished fifth) have so little in common that it would seem justifiable to consider them as " irreconcilably remote ", were it not that the imagination of a real artist is capable of overcoming even this obstacle. On the other hand, one should not forget that the progressions of the Neapolitan sixth chord to the tonic chord, ₦—I [or i], and to the dominant chord, II—V [i.e. progressions of a minor second or augmented fourth] are common.

Much in these examples is imperfect. Trying to improve some of their shortcomings might be an interesting exercise. It is, however, doubtful whether the natural cause of their defects can be eliminated; they are only exercises in harmonic progressions for which there is no compositional stimulation. Good part leading will always be of great assistance. This refers especially to the main voices, the outer voices—soprano and bass; difficult and even unmelodious progressions will better be hidden in the middle voices—chromatic and quasi-diatonic progressions can soften many a harsh connection by their melodious qualities. The outer voices are also helpful in introducing substitutes—transformations and vagrant chords—if their directional tendencies are carefully observed. The final cadence must not be too short, especially if it has been preceded by remote deviations. Common natural chords are most effective for transitions, but in the examples even Neapolitan sixth chords, augmented triads and $^6_5$-chords, and diminished 7th chords have been treated like common chords.

# CHAPTER IX

## CLASSIFICATION OF RELATIONSHIP

ACCORDING to the practice of composers of the tonal period up to and including most of the 19th century, the relationships between tonalities can be classified as follows:

MAJOR

1. Direct and Close: [as related to T],
   SD, D, sm, m (Chapter III, p. 26 ff, Ex. 47).
2. Indirect but Close:
   A. Through Common Dominant:
      (1) t, sd, v (Chapter VII, p. 51 ff, Exs. 72–76).
      (2) SM, M (Chapter VIII, p. 58, Ex. 77).
   B. Through Proportional Transposition:
      ♭M, ♭SM (Chapter VIII, p. 60, Ex. 77).
3. Indirect:
   ♭m, ♭sm, MM, Mm, ♭smSM, ♭smsm (Chapter VIII, p. 61, Ex. 78).
4. Indirect and Remote:
   Np, dor, S/T, ♭MD, ♭mv (Chapters VIII and IX, p. 66 ff, Exs. 80–83).
5. Distant:
   MSM, Msm, SMM, SMm, SMSM, SMsm, S/TM, S/Tm, S/TSM, S/Tsm, ♭mvM, ♭mvm, ♭mvSM, ♭mvsm, ♭mM, ♭mm, ♭mSM, ♭msm, ♭smM, ♭smm (Chapter IX).

Class 1 is called DIRECT AND CLOSE because all these regions have five (or six) tones in common with **T**.

Class 2 is called INDIRECT BUT CLOSE because all these regions are closely related to the regions of Class 1 or to tonic minor, and have three or four tones in common with **T**.

Class 3 is called INDIRECT because all these regions are more distant than Class 2, upon which their relationship is based, and the number of tones in common with **T** is negligible.

**MM** and **Mm**, **♭smSM** and **♭smsm** are very distant on the chart,[1] but if enharmonically changed they sound like

[1] See p. 20.

more closely related regions. **MM** and **Mm** sound like ♭**SM** and ♭**sm** (in terms of their tonics in **C** major, like **G♯** and **g♯**= **A♭** and **a♭**); similarly, ♭**smSM** (**F♭**) and ♭**smsm** (**f♭**) sound like **M** (**E**) and **m** (**e**).

Structurally this means that these rather distant regions may be reached either by way of the flats or by way of the sharps, respectively—or, so to speak, either clockwise or counter-clockwise in the circle of fifths. Thereafter they can be enharmonically changed (see the second and third endings to Ex. 77e, pp. 59-60).

Class 4 is called INDIRECT AND REMOTE because these five regions are connected in the following manner:

Dorian (**dor**) is subdominant's submediant minor (**SDsm**);

Supertonic (**S/T**) is subdominant's submediant major (**SDSM**);

Neapolitan (**Np**) is subdominant minor's submediant major (**sdSM**);

Flat major mediant's dominant (♭**MD**) is subdominant's subdominant (**SDSD**);

Flat minor mediant's " five-minor " (♭**mv**) is subdominant minor's subdominant minor (**sdsd**).

In 19th century music, these extremely remote regions, and most of the regions of Class 5 (DISTANT) customarily appear in the *Durchführungen* (developments or elaborations)[1]. But ♭**MD** (A♭ in the tonality of B♭ major) appears in the contrasting middle section of the cavatina, " Voi che sapete ", from *The Marriage of Figaro*[2] (Ex. 81a). This same region is also employed within the first statement of the main theme (in substution for the usual II) in Beethoven's Sonata, Op. 53 (Ex. 81b). See also in his Sonata, Op. 31/1, the relation F to G major (Ex. 81c).

---

[1 Schoenberg's reasons for using the term *Durchführung*, rather than " development ", " elaboration " or " working out ", will be found on p. 145.]

[2] The difficulty of finding a second illustration of this kind, coupled with some other circumstances (for instance, the long roundabout return to the tonic), suggests the following hypothesis: the page, Cherubino, accompanies himself and is also the author of the poem. Has he not also composed the music? Did not Mozart by such extravagant features hint at Cherubino's professional imperfections?

a) Mozart: Marriage of Figaro (Voi, che sapete)

b) Beethoven: Sonata, Op. 53

c) Beethoven: Sonata, 31/1

An example of **S/T** is to be found in the *Durchführung*[1] of Beethoven's Sonata, Op. 2/3, in C major (Ex. 82).

**Np** is usually approached through **sd** or through the augmented $\frac{6}{5}$ of Ħ. Though this region is fairly distant, an extended episode often takes place within it. Examples of this kind are frequent, as, for instance, the two following cases from Beethoven Piano Sonatas.

*a)* Beethoven: Sonata, Op.2/2, Rondo

[1] cf. p. 69.

*b)* Beethoven: Sonata, Op. 7, Rondo

Tonalities or regions whose tonics are a major or minor second, a diminished fifth or an augmented fourth distant from the tonic are less frequently considered as related by the composers of the period mentioned above.[1]

The relation **Msm** (mediant major's submediant minor)— c♯ in C major or e in E♭ major—takes place in the Eroica, ms. 284, in the *Durchführung* (see Ex. 149, p. 155).

Even more interesting cases can be found in the works of Brahms, for instance in the F minor Piano Quintet. In the recapitulation, the first subordinate theme (ms. 201), which in the first division stood on **sm** (c♯), ms. 35, should have been transposed to tonic minor (f). Instead it is transposed to **Msm** (f♯). In the 'Cello Sonata in F major, Op. 99, one is surprised to find the second movement in F♯ major, only to discover later that F major and f minor are contrastingly connected with F♯ (G♭) major and f♯ minor in all four movements. What makes these Brahms examples so striking is that most of them do not occur in *Durchführungen* but in place where " establishing " conditions exist—in regions, that is.

MINOR

The evaluation of the regions in the minor requires a different yardstick, because a natural dominant is lacking, and the two substitute tones of the ascending scale increase the number of possible harmonies.

Relations derived from the natural tones of the descending scale differ from those of the major in that the fifth degree (v) is not a dominant, while the mediant (**M**, relative major) exerts an influence similar to a dominant. Besides, there is no Dorian region on II (because of its diminished triad) comparable to that in the major; but the region on VII (**subT**) often functions like a dominant to **M**.

Relations derived from the ascending scale contain a functional dominant (**D**), but the subdominant, though here a major chord, seems a greater departure from the tonic region than the subdominant in major.

[1] See p. 65.

The indirectly related regions:

**m, sm, ♯m, ♯M, ♯sm, ♯SM, Np, Dsm, DSM, subT, SD**

derive from

**M, SM,  D,  D,  T,   T,  SM,  D,   D,    M,   sd.**

Two remarkable, if not exceptional, examples from Beethoven's String Quartets, Op. 59/2 in E minor (3rd movement) and Op. 132 in A minor (4th movement), can be understood as a cadence and half cadence, respectively, to V of **M**.

*a)*   Beethoven: Quartet, Op. 59/2, 3rd Movement

*b)*   Beethoven: Quartet, Op. 132, 4th Movement

The evaluation of the more remote regions will best be based on mediant (relative major). (Compare Ex. 79 and later examples, especially analyses of *Durchführungen*—see p. 145 ff.).

Should a modulation have to pass through two regions which have no common natural chords (such as **v** and **♯M**). it is best to interpolate a few chords of an intermediate region (in this case, **D**).

## CLASSIFICATION OF REGIONS IN MINOR

1. Close: M, T, v, sd (Chapter IV, p. 31 ff., Ex. 49).
2. Indirect but Close: D, SM (Chapter IV, p. 32 ff., Ex. 49).
3. Indirect: m, sm, SD (Chapter VIII, p. 63, Ex. 79).
4. Indirect and Remote: ♯sm, ♯SM, ♯m, ♯M, subT, subt, Np (Chapter VIII, p. 64, Ex. 79).
5. Distant: All other regions.

# CHAPTER X

## EXTENDED TONALITY

THE COMPOSERS of the Romantic period believed that music should " express " something. As so often in preceding periods, extramusical tendencies, such as poetic and dramatic subjects, emotions, actions, and even philosophical problems of *Weltanschauung* (philosophy of life) had become influential. These tendencies caused changes in every feature of the musical substance. Alterations in the constitution of chords decisively changed the intervals of the melodies and also resulted in richer modulations; the rhythms and dynamics of the accompaniment, and even of the melody, symbolized their extramusical objects instead of deriving from purely musical stimuli. The origin of these new features may be debatable aesthetically, if not psychologically; however, whatever the source of the musical inspiration may have been, it resulted in great developments.

In descriptive music the background, the action, the mood and the other features of the drama, poem or story become incorporated as constituent and formative factors in the musical structure. Their union thereafter is inseparable. Neither the text nor the music conveys its full significance if detached from its companion. Their union is an amalgamation comparable to an alloy whose components can be separated only by complicated processes.

Drama and poetry are greatly inspiring to a composer. But much of what they evoke on the one hand, they revoke on the other. A melody, if it followed the dictates of its musical structure alone, might develop in a direction different from that in which a text forces it. It might become shorter or longer, produce its climax earlier or later—or dispense with it entirely —require less striking contrasts, much less emphasis, or much less accentuation. Besides, the text is frequently so overwhelming in itself as to conceal the absence of value in a melody.

These extramusical influences produced the concept of extended tonality. Remote transformations and successions of harmonies were understood as remaining within the tonality. Such progressions might or might not bring about modulations or the establishment of various regions. They function chiefly as enrichments of the harmony and, accordingly, often appear in a very small space, even in a single measure. Though referring them to regions may sometimes facilitate analysis, their functional effect is, in many cases, only passing, and temporary.

In the beginning of the Prelude to *Tristan*, V of **a** minor is followed by two modulating sequences (see Ex. 85a), the last of which prepares for the recurrence of the opening V (ms. 16). In 85b, from Strauss' *Salome*, ms. 3 (at +) a harmony appears which seems difficult to explain. But if one considers the **e♮** as a mere passing note, connecting the **f** with the **d♯** (**e♭**), it becomes clear that it is a diminished seventh chord of **♯♯**, sounding much more remote here.

a) Wagner: Prelude to Tristan

b) Strauss: Salome (after ♯257)

x) quasi-passing over f♭ (e♮) to e♭.

However, far-reaching deviations, resulting from remote progressions, occur frequently in Brahms. In the C minor String Quartet, Op. 51, first movement, the contrasting middle section ends on the tone **f♯** (ms. 21), which must undoubtedly be analyzed as V of dominant's mediant minor (Dm), an extremely remote point scarcely appropriate to reintroduce I of **c** minor. A little unaccompanied fragment then serves as a retransition to **t** (Ex. 86a).

If Brahms were not a profound thinker and a great virtuoso in the treatment of harmonic problems, he would simply have repeated this procedure in the recapitulation. But in order eventually to recapitulate the subordinate theme in **t** he shifts the a¹ section[1], ms. 23, to **sd**, a fifth below (86b). Accordingly the tone which precedes the little fragment of ms. 22 should have been transposed similarly, i.e. to **B**. But instead of that he arrives at **E**, the V of **♯sm**, and requires two more modulatory measures for the introduction of **sd**.

Brahms: String Quartet, Op. 51

Brahms gave similar advice to young composers. Thus, in Ex. 87a, ms. 2, he recommended, instead of a simple repetition, the replacement of the last chord by a minor triad which could be employed in the *Durchführung* to change to the flat keys (" zu den B-Tonarten ", he said).

---

[1] Cf. p. 98 n.

In the works of earlier composers many passages of extended tonality are to be found. Ex. 88 and Ex. 89 from Bach's G minor Organ Fantasy and from the Chromatic Fantasy are composed of such remotely related transformations.

*a)* Bach: Organ Fantasy in G minor

*b)*

Bach: Chromatic Fantasy (D minor)

Deviation into remote regions often occurs in descriptive music, even in "establishing" [expository] sections. Songs, operas, choral works and symphonic poems take advantage of the emotional expressiveness of extravagant modulations. See, for instance, the two examples, 90 and 91—"Auf dem Flusse" by Schubert and "Der Tod, das ist die kuhle Nacht" by Brahms—and the little recitative from the St. Matthew Passion, Ex. 92, to the words "Ach, Golgotha".

Schubert: Auf dem Flusse

Brahms: Op. 96, No. 1

Bach: St. Matthew Passion
Ach Golgotha!

92.

The inclusion of the Neapolitan sixth within the main themes of the Beethoven String Quartets Op. 59/2 in E minor and Op. 95 in F minor (Exs. 93, 94) certainly should be regarded as extended tonality. Even richer in the inclusion of regions within a main theme are the first movement of the String

Quintet in G major, Op. 111 (Ex. 95) and the main theme of
the Piano Concerto in D minor (Ex. 96), both by Brahms.

T I   IV   II   III   VI
(sm) IV   V   I

T VI
M IV   II   I⁶₄   V   II   IV

T VI   III   VI   II   I⁶₄   V   VII
M IV   I   IV

T IV   {VI
(t) {VI   II   V

Brahms: Concerto in D minor, Op. 15

Enriched harmony makes for variety, especially when repetitions threaten to produce monotony. One of the most interesting examples of this kind can be found in Schubert's song, "Sei mir gegrüsst" (Ex. 97). In his songs Schubert always expresses and intensively illustrates the mood and character of the poem. In "Der Lindenbaum", "Die Krähe", "Letzte Hoffnung", Erlkönig", "Gretchen am Spinnrad", for instance, the piano illustrates, respectively, the sound of the wind, the flight of the crow, the falling of leaves, the galloping horse, and the sound of the spinning wheel. He achieves even more through strange harmonic progressions, as in "Der Wegweiser" (Ex. 98), or abrupt modulations, as ms. 18 of "In der Ferne" (Ex. 99) and in "Erlkönig" (Ex. 100).

Schubert: Sei mir gegrüsst

*a)* Refrain: ms. 13—18, 23—28, 39—44, 54—59, 72—77, 91—96

Strophes 1 and 2 (ms. 9—12, 19—22)

*b)*

Strophes 3 and 5 (ms. 30—38, 61—71)

*c)*

Schubert: In der Ferne

But in "Sei mir gegrüsst" (Ex. 97) the procedure is very different. Here the piano style, unchanged in general throughout the whole piece, does not illustrate at all, but closely resembles a guitar accompaniment. The refrain, "sei mir gegrüsst", appears at the end of each strophe, a total of six times in only 100 measures. This would be extremely monotonous were it not that far-reaching changes in the harmony make every repetition an interesting variation.

"Variation is that kind of repetition which changes some

of the features of a unit, etc., but preserves others."[1]  Obviously whole sets of variations, which often repeat their model ten times or more, would annoy instead of please if they merely applied changes of piano style, as is the case in some of Handel's variations.  But variations by Haydn, as, for example, Op. 76/3 (Emperor Quartet), 2nd movement, are based in many instances on enrichment of the harmony.[2]

101. Haydn: Quartet, Op.76/3, 2nd Movement

a) Theme

b) Var. IV

---

[1] Arnold Schoenberg: *Models for Beginners in Composition*, G. Schirmer, Inc.
[2] In *Models* instruction is given for enriching the harmony by inserted additions (p. 13–14).

Beethoven, in his three large sets of variations for piano; the 15 Variations, Op. 35 (Eroica), the 32 Variations in C minor, and the 33 Diabelli Variations, Op. 120, similarly, but much more far-reachingly, varies his harmony by using substitutions and transformations (sometimes remote ones) and passing through various regions. This is most significant in the Diabelli Variations, which, in respect of its harmony, deserves to be called the most adventurous work of Beethoven.

Some of the progressions in this work are difficult to analyse in terms of regions, for instance, mss. 9–12 in Var. 15 (Ex. 102a)—substituting for the original sequence (Ex. 103a)—and the corresponding units, mss. 9–12 and 25–28, in Var. 20 (Ex. 102b and 102c). The treatment of diminished 7th chords in Var. 20 (at +) corresponds to the viewpoint of former theorists who simply said: "a diminished 7th chord can precede and follow every harmony." It must not be overlooked that the harmony, besides providing structural advantages, is also capable of producing stimulating means of expression. Under such uncontrollable circumstances analysis has to resign in favour of faithful confidence in the thinking of a great composer.

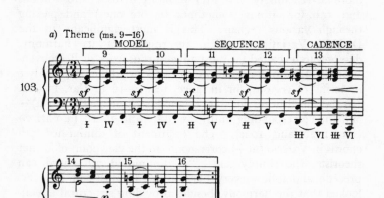

*h)* Var. XI

*i)* Var. XII

*j)* Var. II

*k)* Var. III

*"a"-section is only 15 measures; MODEL begins in ms. 8 instead of 9.

MODEL                                    "SEQUENCE"

*l)* Var. IV

*n*) Var. V    MODEL    "SEQUENCE"

*o*) Var. V

In this work one result of extended tonality is illustrated by the numerous harmonic variations of a segment of four measures. It is the aforementioned segment of mss. 9–12 in the theme, consisting of the progression ~~I~~–IV (9), its repetition (10), and their sequence ~~II~~–V, ~~II~~–V (11-12) (see Ex. 103a). These progressions in the " a " section[1] lead through ~~III~~–VI, etc., to V (16). Curiously, in the " a¹ " section—mss. 25–28 (Ex. 103b)—the same progressions by way of V end on the tonic.

In some of the variations (1, 2, 3, 8, etc.) the initial progression of mss. 9–10 is preserved in both " a " and " a¹ "; but instead of the sequence II–V of mss. 11–12 there appears in " a " of Var. 1, IV–♭VII (Ex. 103c), and in " a¹ " of Var. 1, ~~VI~~–II (Ex. 103d); in Var. 2, ~~VII~~–III (Ex. 103e); in Var. 3, IV–V (103f). The progressions of mss. 25–26 are always repeated here (without much change) in mss. 27–28, with the exception of Var. 3, where mss. 27–28 substitutes ~~II~~–V for IV–V, and Var. 8 (Ex. 103g), where ~~VII~~–III is followed by ~~II~~–I. Similar deviations occur in other variations, e.g., Vars. 11 and 12.

In Vars 1–3 the cadence to the dominant in " a " starts on III (ms. 13), and the cadence to the tonic in " a¹ " starts on V (ms. 29) [see Ex. 103d, e, f]. The connection between the ending of the sequential segment (ms. 12) and the beginning of the cadence is often surprising, as, for instance, in Var. 1 (Ex. 103c)—♭VII–~~III~~ (dim. 7th). In other cases ms. 9 is replaced by ~~III~~–VI (Vars. 4 and 7) [Ex. 103l, m].

The cadence to V in Var. 4 starts on a chromatic passing ~~IV~~ (Ex. 103l). Var. 5 deviates extensively from the original progressions in that mss. 9–10, with incomplete chords, builds a two-measure model (III–~~VII~~) freely sequenced (ms. 11–12) by ~~VII~~–~~III~~ (Ex. 103n). In the same variation the sequence in ms. 27–28 proceeds through ♭VI to the Neapolitan triad on ~~II~~ (Ex. 103*o*).

Another remote variation occurs in ms. 9–12 of Var. 7 (Ex. 103m), where mss. 10 and 12 are only free melodic repetitions of mss. 9 and 11 respectively; ~~III~~–VI is followed by IV–~~IV~~₆, and ~~VII~~ (dim. 7th)–~~VII~~ (art. dom.) by III–~~VII~~.

Now follow some examples from contemporaries and

[1 " a "=expository section; " a¹ "=recapitulatory section.]

successors of Wagner. The motto-like introduction to the second movement of Dvorak's Symphony, "From the New World", can easily be understood as remaining within the tonic region.

Dvorak: E minor Symphony, Largo

Ex. 105, from the second movement of Grieg's 'Cello Sonata, includes, among its many passing harmonies, a number of transformations, passing notes and suspensions, some of them unresolved (at +). But it is definitely in the tonic region.

Grieg: 'Cello Sonata, 2nd Movement

Ex. 106, the Adagio from Bruckner's 7th Symphony, also in the tonic region, likewise contains passing harmonies, passing notes and suspensions.

Bruckner: Symphony No.7, Adagio

Ex. 107, a quotation from *Karwoche* (Holy Week) by Hugo
Wolf—who was one of the most prominent followers of Wagner's achievements in expression, musical illustration and
harmony—is similar in style to many other songs by this
composer. The progressions in this example are better understood if analysed partly in the submediant region. The **f♭** in
ms. 1(+) is a free suspension and does not constitute a harmony
different from that of I. Such "non-constitutional" tones
are characteristic of this period.

Ex. 108 is from Bizet's *Carmen*. Bizet is one of those composers whose rich harmony does not derive from a precon-
ceived scheme of modulation. It is, in other words, not an
embellishment, but it is conditioned by the nature of his
melodies. It can be analysed in the tonic region (**t**), but some
of the progressions are more convincingly presented in mediant
(**M**). Curiously, the tonic harmony does not come before
ms. 13, and, more unusually, it comes here in root position,
as a result of the doubling of the voice melody in the accompaniment (mss. 8–12). Normally, after the Neapolitan (ms. 11)
the $^6_4$-chord can be expected, followed by a dominant on the
same bass tone. Here the voice, leaping up to the **f♯**, forms,
together with the **d**, a kind of inverted pedal on **d–f♯**, below
which the bass proceeds as the true continuation of the melody
toward a pseudo-cadence to I.

The example from César Franck's Symphony (109) is characteristic of the time in which it was written. It is a typical case of chromatic ascent or descent based less on the relations of the main harmonies than on the multiple meaning of diminished 7th chords and other vagrants. Still, an analysis according to **sm** and **m** presents the relation to **t.** The tones marked (+) are best considered as passing melody tones.

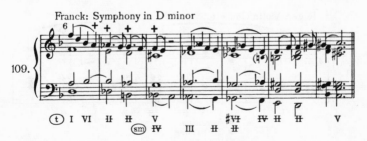

In Ex. 110, the first four measures express I in mss. 1 and 2 and VI in mss. 3 and 4, through the combination of two melody lines without the addition of complete harmonies. In ms. 5 II is incomplete and becomes complete only in ms. 6, also by melodic progression.

Similarly, Ex. 111, though without complete harmonies, distinctly passes through two (or three) regions. The music of Max Reger, like that of Bruckner and Mahler, is little known outside Germany. But his music is rich and new, through his application to "absolute" music of Wagner's achievements in the realm of harmony. Because these were invented for dramatic expression, the application of these procedures in this way provoked an almost "revolutionary" movement among Wagner's successors.

Nine examples from Wagner's operas—probably not the most characteristic ones—illustrate non-modulatory procedures within a tonality. While in classical music many essential changes seldom occur in one measure, Ex. 112a shows the novelty of this procedure by the use of numerous transformed degrees. In 112b, leading to **D**, the essential change occurs at + in ms. 10.

Even richer is Ex. 113; this almost suggests a modulation and remodulation,[1] when in ms. 4 it arrives at ♭**mM**, which must be classified as [5], i.e. Distant.[2]

[1 i.e. modulation back.]
[2 See Classification of Relationship, Chapter IX.]

In Ex. 114 this modulatory contrasting middle section contains two sequences; the same degree numbers appear in every phrase. This modulation is also classified as ⑤.

[*N.B.* **t/T** means tonic minor *or* tonic major.]

The first 24 measures of Ex. 115a remain, in spite of some transformed degrees, close to **T** (or **t**). But the closing segment (115b) modulates very fast to **SMsm**, V–I, Class ⑤, which, perforce, one could register as **SM** (III–VI).

It is advantageous to register Ex. 116 in several regions because the progression in mss. 1–2 is in **S/T**: II (Neap.)–V, similar to **T**: II (Neap.) –V at the end.

Die Walküre: Wotans Abschied

Even in a melody with popular appeal, Ex. 117, the tonality is fairly far extended. Such deviations from simplicity were obstacles for Wagner's contemporaries.

Ex. 118, from "*Die Meistersinger*", is based on a change between **T** and **sm**. So much of it refers to **sm** that one would be inclined to consider it in **g** minor, were the ending in ms. 11 not distinctly on V of **B**♭.

Ex. 119, from *Tristan*, is one of those Wagnerian melodies which are built by quasi-sequential repetitions of a short phrase. It is analysed as being in B minor in spite of the F minor-like progression Ⅱ̶ (Neap.)–V, because this method offers the opportunity of analysing the last phrase (mss. 7–8) as an ending on **v**, substituting for an ending on V. The progressions in the second (mss. 3–4) and third (mss. 5–6) phrases are better called "quasi-Neapolitan" (Ⅱ̶–V) because the harmonies in mss. 3 and 5 are not major chords.

Analysis of Ex. 120a reveals that it is less modulatory than
it seems at first glance. It is only the section mss. 6–17 which,
deviating from **t,** moves through **sm** to **♯m** and (mss. 11–14)
to **♯M**. The progressions in mss. 11 and 12 are explained in
120b as sequences of two transformations of II, also transposed
to III (120c) and VI (120d). If mss. 13 were also a sequence,
it would appear like 120e; instead, two chromatically gliding
diminished 7th chords (used melodically rather than functionally) are connected with I of ♯M, equivalent to ♯III of **t** in
ms. 14. This measure, despite the melodic changes, is analysed
as two forms of one and the same degree, i.e., the 9th of the
diminished 7th chord (f♭) descends and the 7th (d♭) ascends
(through d♮) to the octave (e♭) (Ex. 120f). (Such a procedure
is not infrequent in Wagner, as illustrated in 120g, a form of the
*Rheintöchter-Motiv* (Rhinemaidens' motive) from *Siegfried*.) The
eighth-note figure in mss. 17–24 (120a) is played in unison by
the strings without harmonic accompaniment. Evidently
such a passage would not be logical in Wagner's style without
an intelligible relation to a tonality. Here a rather convincing
attempt has been made to reveal this relation as two transformations of ♁ (mss. 18–22) followed by a cadence (mss. 23–
25).

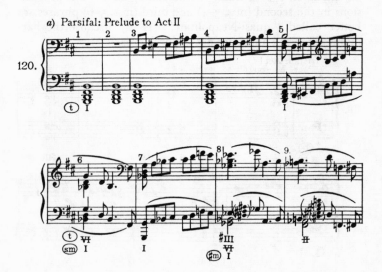

*a)* Parsifal: Prelude to Act II

120.

Extended tonality is also characteristic of my first period (1896–1906); fragments of two songs from Op. 6 are analysed here. At first glance Ex. 121 looks as if it were extremely modulatory. But analysis shows that changes of regions occur only in ms. 3 (♭**SM**), 5 (♭**M**), 6 (♭**m**) and 9—back to ♭**SM**, on whose tonic this section later ends. The apparently free passing notes and suspensions (marked +) are merely melodic but not harmonic. The harmony at " a " (ms. 1) is to be understood as an imperfect form of a 9th chord on V (Ex. 121a). It reappears similarly in ms. 7. Ex. 121b explains the progression IV–**H** of ♭**SM** as changing the roots of one diminished 7th chord, a procedure which is discussed in my *Harmonielehre*, Ex. 304[1]. Similarly, the main theme of my *Kammersymphonie* is introduced by multiple root reference of a diminished 7th chord (121c).

Schoenberg: Der Wanderer, Op. 6, No. 8

+) passing notes or free suspensions.

121.

---

[1] Used without acknowledgement by A. E. Hull.

Ex. 122 is characterized by a number of far-reaching transformations with multiple meanings. The examples, a, b, c and
d explain mss. 11–12, 13, 20 and 21 respectively as transformations and substitutions of 9th chords on **b♭**. The enharmonization of many of these notes somewhat obscures this fact. The
5th (f) is often replaced by f♯, but in ms. 20 by f♭ (e♮) and in
21 by both f♯ and f♭. In ms. 22, Ex. 122d, the root is omitted
and the 7th is in the bass.

Perhaps the most interesting feature of this song, as mentioned
in my *Harmonielehre*, is that the tonic, E♭, does not appear
throughout the whole piece; I call this " schwebende Tonali-
tät " (suspended tonality). Many parts of the song must be
analysed in **sm**. The contrasting modulatory section, mss. 32–
41, uses for a retransition [i.e. modulation back], the segment
mss. 5–10 in mss. 42–47. This is analysed in 122e in **sm** and
**subT**. It begins (in ms. 42) and ends (45–46) at the same
chords as mss. 5 and 8–9 respectively. The fine point is that
this similarity is produced in spite of the transposition of the
melody a half-step higher (mss. 42–44). Accordingly all
degrees are one step higher.

122.    Schoenberg: Lockung, Op.6, No.7

Analysis of ms. 42–45

The ear of the contemporary musician and music lover is no longer disturbed by far-reaching deviations from diatonic harmonies. This was an obstacle to the contemporaries of Mozart, who called his C major String Quartet the " Dissonance " Quartet. It was again an obstacle to the contemporaries of Wagner, Mahler and Strauss and will remain so for some time to come. But time heals all wounds—even those inflicted by dissonant harmonies.

# CHAPTER XI

THE FORMS for which harmony progressions are recommended in the following chapter are described in Arnold Schoenberg: *Models for Beginners in Composition* (G. Schirmer, N.Y.). Thus all the advice given here refers to the school-forms constructed for the sake of practice. A school-form is an abstraction which differs, often considerably, from reality. For this reason these studies must be complemented by analysis of masterworks. The progressions recommended here will provide for the following forms or formal requirements: sentence, period, codetta, contrasting middle section, transition, sequence, *Durchführung* (elaboration or development), introduction and other so-called " free " forms.

SENTENCE

The school-form for the sentence (eight measures) begins with a two-measure unit, followed by a repetition (mss. 3–4) which can be a sequence or else a more or less contrasting repetition. The sixth measure will be a sequence of the fifth, and mss. 7 and 8 will be cadences to various degrees.

The first unit (mss. 1–2) may consist of two harmonies: I–V, I–IV, I–VI, I–III, I–II;
or of three harmonies:
I–IV–V, I–VI–V, I–II–V, I–V–I, etc.

Similarly I–IV, etc., can be extended; e.g. I–III–IV, I–VI–IV; or I–III–VI, I–V–VI; or I–VII–III (III), I–II–III; or I–VI–II, I–IV–II, etc.

There may also be four or more harmonies in this unit.

The second unit (mss. 3–4) may be a mere interchange of the harmonies of the first, by reversing their order. This method is seldom applicable if there are more than two harmonies.

A few examples of mss. 1–4 follow:

| | First unit | Second unit |
|---|---|---|
| (a) | I–V | V–I |
| (b) | | II–VI |
| (c) | | III–VII |
| (d) | | VI–III, etc. |
| (e) | I–IV | IV–I |
| (f) | | II–V |
| (g) | | III–VI |

|     | *First unit* | *Second unit* |
|-----|--------------|---------------|
| (h) |              | VII–III, etc. |
| (i) | I–VI         | II–VII        |
| (j) |              | III–I         |
| (k) |              | IV–II, etc.   |
| (l) | I–III        | IV–VI, etc.   |
| (m) | I–II         | IV–V          |
| (n) |              | V–VI          |
| (o) |              | II–III, etc.  |
| (p) | I–V–I        | V–I–V, etc.   |

The third unit (ms. 5) and its sequence (ms. 6) will, for the sake of practice, preferably avoid repetition of a preceding progression.

An eight-measure sentence might be based on progressions like the following:

| ms. | 1–2 | 3–4 | 5 | 6 | 7 | 8 |
|-----|-----|-----|---|---|---|---|
| (a) | I–V | V–I | VI–II | VII–III | VI–IV | I⁶₄–V–I |
| (b) | Alternative | | | | I–VI–IV–II | I⁶₄–V–I |
| (c) | Same 6 ms. cadencing to **D**: | | | | {T VI–II̶ | V } |
| | | | | | {D II–V | I } |
| (d) | Alternative: | | | | {T VI–II̶I̶–VI–II̶ | V } |
| | | | | | {D II–V̶I̶–II–V | I } |
| (e) | Same 6 ms. cadencing to **m**: | | | | **m**VI–II | I⁶₄–V–I |

Here follow harmonic excerpts of sentences from Beethoven's Piano Sonatas:

| | ms. | 1–2 | 3–4 | 5 | 6 | 7 | 8 |
|--|-----|-----|-----|---|---|---|---|
| Op. 2/1 1st mvmt., f minor: | | I | V | I | V | I–II | V(D) |
| Op. 2/3, 1st mvmt., C major: | | I–V | V–I | I–V | I–V | I–II | V–I |

Op. 7, 2nd mvmt., C major:

| ms. | 1 | 2 | 3 | 4 | 5 | 6 | 7 | 8 |
|-----|---|---|---|---|---|---|---|---|
| | I–V | V–I | I–II̶ | II̶–V | I–V–I | II | V | I |

## PERIOD

The school-form for the period consists of two segments of four measures each. The first, the antecedent, may end on V, either through mere interchange (e.g. I–V–I–V) or in a more elaborate manner, or through a half cadence with or without substitutes (Ex. 123a). In the minor, the procedure is similar (124a).

The second segment, the consequent (mss. 5–8), may repeat part of the antecedent, and usually concludes with a perfect cadence to I, V, or III in major (123b), or I, III, V or v in minor (124b).

PERIODS
Antecedents

123.

I    V    I    V    I  I⁶  V  V    I  I⁶    V

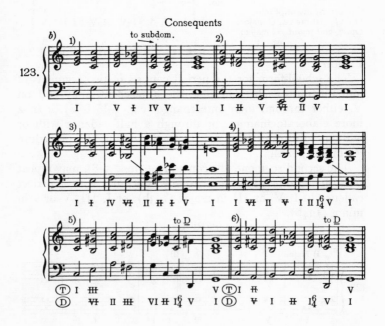

Consequents

## PERIODS: minor
### Antecedents

Here are a few illustrations of periods from Beethoven's Piano Sonatas:

|  | ms. | 1 | 2 | 3 | 4 | 5 | 6 | 7 | 8 |
|---|---|---|---|---|---|---|---|---|---|
|  |  |  | *Antecedent* |  |  |  | *Consequent* |  |  |
| Op. 2/1, 2nd |  |  |  |  |  |  |  |  |  |
| mvmt., F maj.: |  | I | V | I–V–I | V, | I | IV–V–I | IV–I–V | I |
| Op. 2/2, 4th |  |  |  |  |  |  |  |  |  |
| mvmt., A maj.: |  | I | V | I–V–IV | I–V, | I |  |  |  |
|  |  |  |  |  |  | **D**: IV–I | II | I–V | I |
| Op. 7, 4th |  |  |  |  |  |  |  |  |  |
| mvmt. E♭ maj.: |  | V–(I) | V | I–V–I | V, | V–(I) | V | I–II–I–V | I |

## CODETTA

A codetta, as regard its structural functions, is merely a cadence, whatever its motival or thematic implications may be. In classical music its harmonic range comprises all forms from the mere interchange of I–V, etc., to the most remotely enriched cadences. See, for instance, mss. 113–144 in the 1st movement of the Eroica (Ex. 125).

Beethoven: 3ʳᵈ Symphony, 1ˢᵗ Movement, Codetta

125.

\* This is Ⓓ with reference to Ⓣ = E♭

CONTRASTING MIDDLE SECTION

As the middle part of forms which consist of more than two parts, i.e. simple ternary forms—minuets, scherzos, etc.— and other forms consisting of three divisions—sonatas, symphonies, concertos, etc.,—the middle section is supposed to form a contrast to the preceding and the succeeding sections. The harmony plays a decisive role in the production of this contrast. In simple cases a change of region is enough. Thus, as the " a " section presents **T** or **t**, whether it ends on I or on another degree of the scale, the regions of either **D**, **m** or **SD** in major, or **D**, **M** and **v** in minor, are a sufficient contrast. For the region of **D** see Beethoven's Piano Sonata, Op. 2/2, 2nd movement; for **SM**, his Sonata op. 14/1, 2nd movement.

Ex. 126 illustrates progressions for simple as well as more elaborate cases. 126a is a mere interchange of V–I on a pedal (for pedal see p. 137). 126b (I–V, I–V) and c (I–IV–V, I–IV–V) begin on I. Generally the contrasting middle section will begin on a degree other than that used to begin or end the " a " section. Therefore the following progressions (126d–m) begin on V, III, VI, II, IV, and on I–minor, v–minor, IV-minor, flat III and flat VI.

Contrasting Middle Section

126.

In many of these examples mss. 3–4 repeat 1–2 with a slight change required for the introduction of the upbeat harmony, V.[1]

[1 Schoenberg used "upbeat harmony" to describe the penultimate chord leading to the returning tonic, i.e., the " downbeat ".]

The harmony is richer in the following examples taken at random from musical literature. In Schubert's *Morgengruss* (Ex. 127), the movement from **v** to **V** is carried out with substitutes. An example from Chopin's Prelude in Db (Ex.128) passes through **v** to **sm** which finally, as VI of **T**, is followed by V. In Ex. 129 from Brahms' G minor Piano Quartet, Op. 25, the contrasting middle section starts on V and soon moves to **m**, on whose V a little episode is built, repeated with a slight variation on I of **M** which is Ḥ of **T**. The middle part of the Bridal Chorus from Wagner's *Lohengrin* (Ex. 130) after an interchange of IV and V, returns to **SM**, passes again through **T** and, in its last segment, proceeds to **M/m**. Ex. 131, from my *Kammersymphonie* (middle part of the Adagio section) offers some difficulty because of the double meaning of the tones marked +. The tones on the third quarters of mss. 2 and 3 and the B♮ on the fourth quarter of ms. 2 are anticipations of the harmony on the following beats. The whole segment is based on the frequent interchange of **D** and **v**.

Brahms: Piano Quartet in G minor, Op. 25 (3rd Movement: E♭maj.)

129.

(harmonic excerpt)

Episode

Wagner: Bridal Chorus, Lohengrin

130.

Schoenberg: Kammersymphonie, Adagio

131.

SEQUENCE

A sequence is an exact repetition of a segment transposed to another degree. A true transposition to another degree will express another region, thus producing a modulation. So-called tonal sequences, using only the diatonic tones, are imperfect sequences because they necessarily replace major chords by minor and vice-versa (Ex. 132).

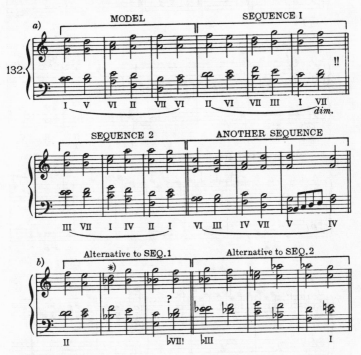

The sequence offers the technical advantage of being a repetition and yet producing a slight contrast by the use of another region. For this reason it has been used abundantly by almost all the great composers. It was especially the sequential transposition within the structure of a theme, from a tonic to a Dorian region,—used sometimes even by great composers (see, for example, Beethoven's C major Symphony, Schubert's Trio in B♭ and C major Quintet, Ex. 133),—which seemed hackneyed to later composers. Composers of Brahms'

school avoided not only this kind of sequence but every unchanged repetition, no matter in what region.

The progressions for contrasting middle sections in Ex. 134 consist of sequential (or quasi-sequential) repetition. The ending of the original segment, or MODEL, should introduce or lead to the harmony which begins the sequence. Accordingly, part of the modulation will often occur within the model, as, for instance, in 134d, e, f, g, etc.

For compositional purposes it is often necessary to arrive at the end of a sequence on a definite degree of the scale, for example, in a transition (see p. 139) or for an up-beat harmony before a recapitulation, etc. Hence it is necessary to build the model in a certain manner and to start the sequence on a definite degree. If the model, for example,

| begins on | | | | the sequence will be | |
|---|---|---|---|---|---|
| I (T/t) and ends on | | | II(2nd up), | IV to V | |
| I | ,, | ,, ,, | ♭II(–2nd up), | ♯IV to V (enhar-monic) | |
| I | ,, | ,, ,, | III(3rd up), | ♭III to V | |
| I | ,, | ,, ,, | ♭III(—3rd up), | III to V | |
| I | ,, | ,, ,, | IV(4th up), | II to V | |
| I | ,, | ,, ,, | VI(3rd down), | ♭VII to V | |
| I | ,, | ,, ,, | ♭VI(+3rd down), | VII to V | |
| I | ,, | ,, ,, | VII(2nd down), | ♭VI to V | |
| I | ,, | ,, ,, | ♭VII(+2nd down) | VI to V | |

In Ex. 135 three of the more difficult problems regarding regions are carried out. In 135a the model should end on II, i.e. **dor**, a minor region. If the sequence must really end on **D** this could be an exact sequence except for the last chord. Ex. 135b is remarkable because of the ending on ♭III (I of ♭**M**). The sequence then begins on I of (♮) **M** as Neapolitan of ♭**M**. Ex. 135c begins with an artificial dominant 7th chord on I.

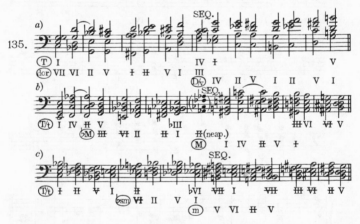

In Ex. 136 sequences on various degrees are shown: major 2nd up (136d and h,) major 2nd down (136g), minor 3rd up (136e and f), minor 3rd down (136a and c), 5th up (136b). The sequence is introduced by a V in 136b, led in as a I to ₶₶

progression in 136c, as a IV–V–VI progression in 136a, by a repetition of the same harmony in 136d, and by interchanging **m** for **M** in minor in 136e. The sequence in 136g becomes more understandable if, eliminating some subordinate tones, one substitutes the roots on which the progressions are based (136h). In 136f the $^6_4$-chords at the beginnings of model and sequence obscure the progressions slightly, but the roots mark them as a deceptive progression, V–VI, in **D**. In 136i the beginning of the sequence does not suggest deviation from **T**; only at the second measure does the change to **S/T** become evident.

*a*) Bach: Brandenburg Concerto No. 2 (F major)

*b*) Beethoven: Sonata Op. 2/3 (C major)

*c*) Beethoven: Sonata Op. 10/1 (C minor)

*d*) Beethoven: Sonata Op. 2/2, Scherzo (A major)

*e*) Tschaikovsky: Symphony No. 6 (B minor)

## VARIATION OF THE SEQUENCE

Of higher value æsthetically are sequences in which variations produce an even stronger effect without endangering the memorability of the model. Slight changes in the part leading, passing notes, chromaticism, suspensions, etc., produce more vital variants of the original. Substitutes and transformations, and especially interpolated chords, are further means to this end. Substitutes and transformations will best be used to make the part leading more effective or convincing.

In Ex. 137, sequences in almost every region have been added to a model I–V. They preserve the I–V of these regions but insert one or more intermediate harmonies. Similarly, other models can be enriched—for instance, I–III, I–IV, I–VI, and I–II; one may also use models consisting of more than two harmonies—for instance, I–IV–V, I–II–V, I–VI–V, I–VI–IV, I–VI–II, etc., or, like the model in 137l, I–V–VI–II. Evidently a model in the middle of a piece can also begin with a degree other than I, as in Ex. 138a and c. In 138b and d these sequences are enriched in the part leading through passing chromatic notes and even through passing transformations. In the examples of 139 the part leading is more elaborately varied. The relation between model and sequence in 140a is closer than the notation reveals.

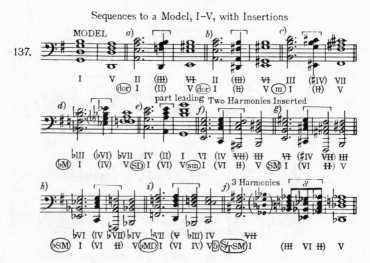

Sequences to a Model, I–V, with Insertions

In Ex. 141 are a few illustrations from musical literature in which the structural advantages of the sequence—namely repetition, harmonic progress and slow development—are achieved without strict sequential treatment of the model. Evidently such deviations can only be used if the substituting progressions are not weaker than those of the original—which is not easy to determine.

*c*) Brahms: Piano Quintet

# PEDAL

A pedal point, a retarding or restraining device of compositional technique, appears in various places. The restraint is produced by one or two voices, which sustain one or two tones, usually root and fifth, while other voices move freely through various harmonies. The conventional rule demands that the sustained voice should begin and end as a consonance; between these consonances, even harmonies which are dissonant to the pedal tone may occur. Generally the sustained note is in the bass. If in another voice, it is called an " inverted " pedal. The general belief that " every " harmony can appear in these circumstances requires a correction. No other harmonies should appear than those consistent with the structural and stylistic conditions of the environment—in other words, only harmonies which would be usable if there were no sustained voices.

Accordingly, from the standpoint of structural functions there is not much interest in pedal points.

If it occurs at the beginning of a piece, the sustained note is usually a pedal on I or V. Here it assists establishment of the tonality by retarding an early modulatory movement. Such pedals can be seen in the following masterpieces: Beethoven's Sonata, Op. 28, 1st and 4th movements; String Quartet, Op. 74, 1st movement; Mozart's E♭ String Quartet, Trio of Minuet; D major Quartet No. 7, Minuet; D major Quartet No. 8, 1st movement; Schubert's A minor String Quartet, Op. 29, 1st movement; Brahms' C minor Quartet, Op. 51, 1st movement.

Here one seldom finds more than an interchange of I–I–IV–V–I; sometimes II, II, VI and IV also appear. II is then generally a diminished 7th chord or an artificial dominant.

In contrasting middle sections (see Beethoven's Sonatas, Op. 2/1, Adagio, and Op. 2/2, Rondo, etc.) before the recapitulation, in transitions (Beethoven's Sonata, Op. 53, 1st movement; Op. 7, 1st movement, etc.) and in *Durchführungen* (cf. p. 145) (Beethoven's Eroica, 1st movement; String Quartet, Op. 74, etc.), the pedal marks the end of the modulatory process. Dwelling on the pedal enhances the expectation of the tonality or region to follow by delaying its appearance. The harmonies here do not differ much from those found over pedals at beginnings of movements, except that they generally begin on a V of a tonality or region and end on a I (or deceptively on VI, IV or II).

In addition, pedals may be found in codettas, episodes and even subordinate themes. Certain exceptional cases should be mentioned: the Prelude to *Das Rheingold*, which is based unchangingly on an E♭ triad; the Fugue of Brahms' *Deutsches Requiem*, and the entire *Durchführung* and Coda of his D minor Violin Sonata, Op. 108, 1st movement, both written over a pedal bass throughout.

But the use of a pedal point to conceal the poverty of the harmony or the absence of a good bass line is not justified. Unfortunately most of the pedal points of mediocre composers are of this kind. This is the poorest form of homophony.

TRANSITION

In larger forms themes in different regions are often connected by means of a transition. In classical music subordinate
themes are seldom to be found in a region more remote than
Class 2 (see p. 68). Transitions therefore are not very complicated harmonically. They are either new themes beginning
at the end of a main theme (Ex. 142) or modulatory transformations in lieu of an ending. (Ex. 143).

In Ex. 142 the procedure with such new themes is illustrated
by one example of Beethoven and three of Brahms. Sequences
and liquidations[1] make the procedure a gradual one. The
Beethoven example (142a) is quite simple. In two of the
Brahms examples (142b and c) the final turn occurs only after
the sequence of an extraordinarily long model (142b) or after
a partial modulatory repetition (142c). Here the final goal is
analysed as **sm**, which is an enharmonization comparable
to that discussed on p. 162. That this analysis is correct,
i.e. that it need not be registered **♯Mm**, is proved in the continuation and at the end of this division of the movement,
where **SM** is presented in flats. The third Brahms example
(142d) takes a detour before arriving at **M**; this, perhaps,
accounts for the deviation into mediant major's Neapolitan,
which enharmonizes to sharp mediant major (**♯M**).

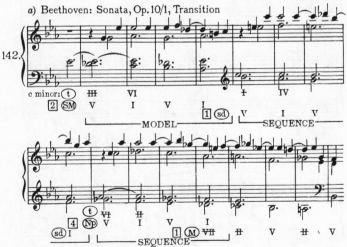

a) Beethoven: Sonata, Op. 10/1, Transition

142.

1 See Arnold Schoenberg, *Models for Beginners*, p. 11.

*b)* Brahms: Symphony No.3, F major: Transition

*c)* Brahms: Piano Quintet in F minor, Op. 34

d) Brahms: Quartet Op.51/2, A minor

Modulatory transformations of the main theme, on the other hand, move without so many intermediate steps directly toward the goal.

Transitions

*a*) Beethoven: Sonata Op. 31/1

*b*) Sonata Op. 53

*c*) Sonata Op. 57

d) Sonata Op.7

Other transitions function as connecting links between codettas (with which a division of a movement ends) and the repetition demanded by repetition marks (first endings of expositions)—see, for instance, Beethoven Sonatas Op. 31/2, Op. 53 and String Quartet Op. 59/3, all 1st movements—or (second endings of expositions) as introductory transitions to the *Durchführung*, or as transitions from the end of the *Durchführung* back to the recapitulation.

As in the recapitulation all the subordinate themes are supposed to appear in the tonic region, a transition would seem superfluous, were it not that the composer knows that the listener likes to hear again valuable material of the first division [exposition]. In most cases there is a turn to the subdominant, followed by a simple transposition leading to V. In other cases, like Beethoven's Quartet Op. 18/6, the Piano Sonata Op. 106, etc., an extended roundabout way is taken to produce a contrast between tonic and tonic. One of the most interesting instances in this respect is illustrated in Ex. 144 from Mozart's G minor Symphony.

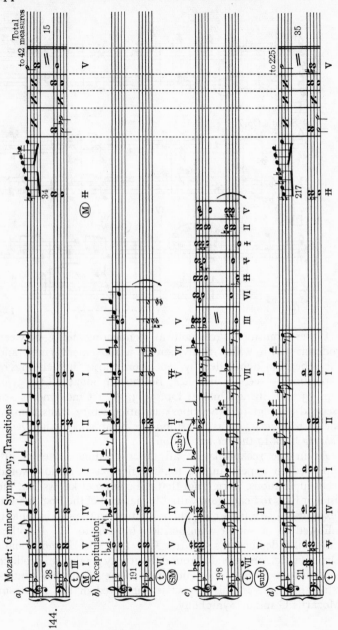

144.

Mozart: G minor Symphony, Transitions

## DURCHFÜHRUNG (ELABORATION)

Almost every larger composition contains one or more divisions which are of modulatory construction. In medium-sized compositions (minuets, scherzos, etc.) this part is best called a *modulatory contrasting (middle) section*. In larger forms, in accommodation to the more complex construction of the first division and its recapitulation—the third division—a more elaborate and more compound contrasting second division is required. This second division is usually called "development", "elaboration", "working-out", etc. There is development everywhere in a piece of music, especially in the first division, where a number of themes are developed from a basic motive. Nothing can remain without being elaborated or worked out. What happens in this second division is something different. Themes of the first division and their derivatives are found in a constant modulatory movement through many and even through remote regions.

This movement through the regions is much better characterized by the term *Durchführung*, which means that the themes which have not modulated in the first division are now *geführt durch*, (led through) contrasting regions in a modulatory procedure.

Bach's modulatory contrasting sections in his larger forms—for instance, Preludes, Toccatas, Gigues, even Fugues, etc.—certainly lead a phrase, a theme, or some other segment of the first section through a number of regions (Ex. 145).

*a)* Bach: Prelude, English Suite II (A minor)

b) Bach: Gigue, Partita VI (E minor)

In comparison, Haydn passes through more regions and more remote ones in the G major (Surprise) Symphony. He includes here even a region which is classified as indirect and remote (**subT**).[1]

[1] Equivalent to ♭**mv**, Class 4.

Haydn: G major Symphony: Durchführung

Even richer than the preceding *Durchführung* is the compass of modulation in the first movement of Mozart's G minor Symphony (Ex. 147). It passes successively through regions classified as close and direct ①, indirect but close ②, indirect ③ and distant⑤. The compass of the last movement is even more remote (Ex. 148).

Mozart: G minor Symphony: Durchführung

Mozart: G minor Symphony 4th Movement

Beethoven's *Durchführungen*, with their dramatic inclinations, often aim for even greater contrasts than structural considerations require. In the Eroica this can best be seen (Ex. 149) in the succession of **sm** (ms. 178), **♯sm** (ms. 181), **mv** (ms. 185) which are classed respectively as ①, ⑤ and ⑤. Moreover, these regions are very distantly related among themselves. If, for instance, the beginning of this segment were the tonic, the sequence in ms. 181 would be a ⑤ relation and, similarly, the same relation would exist in the following sequence. One of the most extravagant ventures occurs when a new theme is placed in **SMm** (ms. 284), followed by a partial repetition in **SMsm** (ms. 292), which are the most distant relations. These same segments are later repeated (mss. 322 and 330) in **t** and **♭M**. The relation between this segment and its repetition is also a very distant one.

Beethoven: Symphony No.3, Durchführung

The richness of Schubert's harmony perhaps marks the actual transition to Wagnerian and post-Wagnerian composers' procedures. In a relatively short *Durchführung* of a String Quartet (!) (Ex. 150) he stays, for longer or shorter periods, in the following regions: **sd**, **sm**, **m**, **sd**, **smsm**, the relations of which are classed respectively ⓵, ⓶, ⓶, ⓵ and ⓹. The **smsm** region (ms. 150) seems more distant because of the somewhat roving modulations in the preceding measures, which define it as derived from **sm**. But an enharmonic change would make it tonic major's mediant (db = c#).

Schubert: String Quartet in A minor, Op. 29 Durchführung

150.

The *Durchführung* of Mendelssohn's Third Symphony in A minor (Ex. 151) is richer in modulation and passes through more remote regions than the first movement of the Fourth Symphony in A major. It starts by considering the tone " e " of the first ending on **v** as the third of I of **♯m** (evaluated as ④) in the second ending. A further modulation to **dor** ④ leads over **subt** ④ to **m** ③, again to **subt** and **sd** Ⅰ followed by **SM** ②, then **subt** and, with roving harmony, to **t**.

Mendelssohn: Symphony No. 3 in A minor

Schumann resembles Mendelssohn in that his modulation is tamer than one would expect from his rich and fluent harmony. Ex. 152 shows that he includes regions of classes [1], [2], and [3], that is **t**, **sd**, **v**, **dor** (all minor), also ♭**M**, ♭**m** and **t**.

Schumann Piano Quintet in E♭

In order to connect the *Durchführung* proper (ms. 77) of the 1st movement of Brahms' 3rd Symphony in F major (Ex. 153) with the second ending of the first division (on **m**), an introductory transition is inserted. The beginning of the *Durchführung* (written as a c♯ minor region in the strings and woodwind) is, as the analysis reveals, an enharmonization of a d♭ minor region (so written in the brass); thus the region is in fact ♭**sm**, not **Mm**, which is rather remote from the **m** of the second ending. For a real understanding of the modulatory procedure it is necessary to " register " the regions according to the way they are introduced. This region (♭**sm**) was introduced by way of the flat regions. This ♭**sm** (ms. 77) and later **subT** (ms. 101) are the only points at which the *Durchführung* settles down for a longish time. Between these two points the harmony is roving, in a circle of fifths, mss. 92–97, or along a chromatic bass line, mss. 98–99. The section from mss. 110 to 112 is analysed as **subT** followed by **subt** to ms. 117, in spite of some incidental deviations (mss. 106–109). The reason for analysing it in this way is the fact that in ms. 120 Brahms introduces a major triad on F, not as a tonic but as a dominant. Accordingly, ms. 117 is considered the turning point to **sd**, of which ms. 120 would be V. This V is now changed in an interesting manner to function as a I in ms. 124, in correspondence to his " motto " motive.

Brahms: Symphony No. 3 in F major: Durchführung

The preceding analyses indicate that while the actual modulation may be either audacious and roving or simple and gradual, regions may be approached whose distance from the tonic region is not always what might be expected. For instance, long segments of a Haydn theme may be based on one or two harmonies only, while the first theme of Schumann's Piano Quintet requires a rich succession of harmonies. Nevertheless, the analyses above show that the distance of regions reached in Haydn's Symphony is greater than that of those in the Schumann example.

The method of evaluation established here can be applied to do justice to composers whose compass of modulation has been underrated, on the one hand, and to those who have been overrated in this respect, on the other hand. The findings might prove in many cases the contrary of what one expected. Thus, for instance, analysis of the Prelude to *Tristan* proves that, on the basis of the interchangeability of **t** and **T**, ♭**M** and ♭**SM** (of **T**) comprise the furthest compass of the modulation, —if one recognizes that those sections which seem to go farther are only roving on the basis of the multiple meaning of a vagrant harmony. Of course this is not a criticism of the beauty of this music.

ROVING HARMONY

Roving harmony was discussed in Chapter I (p. 3). In our analyses of *Durchführungen* some segments have been defined as roving. Extended tonality may contain roving segments, though, on the other hand, various regions may occasionally be firmly established.

Roving harmony need not contain extravagant chords. Even simple triads and dominant 7th chords may fail to express a tonality. See Ex. 154 and the following examples selected from musical literature (Ex. 155 ff.) which are discussed in the following chapter under other considerations.

Beethoven: Sonata Op. 2/2 (C major), 1st movement, 97–109

154.

Roving harmony is based on multiple meaning. Accordingly chords which are vagrants because of their constitution are very effective for this purpose: diminished 7th chords, augmented triads, augmented $\frac{6}{5}$- and $\frac{4}{3}$-chords, Neapolitan triads, other transformations and fourth chords [chords composed of fourths].

## THE SO-CALLED "FREE FORMS"

Introduction, Prelude, Fantasy, Rhapsody, Recitative and others are types of musical organization which previous theorists did not describe but simply called "free", adding, "no special form is adhered to" and "free from formal restrictions". Form to them was not organization but restriction; thus, "free" forms would seem amorphous and unorganized. The cause of this failure of the theorists may be that no two of their "free" forms have a similar structure. But even among forms which are *not* free from formal restrictions—scherzos, rondos, first movements of sonatas and symphonies—it is difficult to find two movements which resemble each other in more than the most primordial outline. It is these differences that make one a work of Beethoven, but another only a work of XY—just as other differences make one creature a man, but another an ape. If composers did not eagerly try to name their works correctly, theorists might also consider those " restricted " forms as unorganized.

Fortunately a composer knows when it is not advisable to begin a piece directly with the subject matter, and when he needs preliminaries. It does not matter whether or not a theorist finds such preparatory sections to be justified. In most cases they are imponderables, and one could scarcely contend that the introduction to Beethoven's Fourth Symphony or Sonata Pathétique could be omitted. Of course, even such things as the first two measures of the Eroica or the first two phrases of the Fifth Symphony would be, strictly speaking, superfluous, were there not such imponderables as a composer's sense of form and expression.

As far as I know, only one scholar has charged himself with the task of investigating the formal conditions for a Prelude: Wilhelm Werker, in his *Studien über die Symmetrie im Bau der Fugen* and *Die Motivische Zusammengehörigkeit der Präludien und Fugen des Wohltemperierten Klaviers von Johann Sebastian Bach* (Breitkopf & Härtel, Leipzig, 1922). Among the problems which he discusses is that of the relationship between a prelude and a fugue; in particular, he reveals that those preludes which he analyses are preparations for the succeeding fugues in the same tonality. The preludes develop out of little germs—motives or phrases—the main features of the themes of their fugues. Though some of Werker's methods may be questionable, there is great merit in his book. Musicology is here what it should be: research into the profundities of musical language.

From the standpoint of structural functions Bach's preludes do not differ essentially from the fugues. It is clear that all the deviations from the respective diatonic scales of each piece should not be considered as modulations. According to the previously given definition of modulation, only a definite departure from a region, together with the appearance of the cadential elements of a new region, constitute a modulation. Substitute tones producing substitute harmonies are to be found in great numbers; real modulations are few. If every tone foreign to the scale were to mean a modulation, how many modulations would there be in the 24th fugue in the first volume (B minor)?

Analysis of other " free " forms offers a different aspect. In all of them a tendency to avoid the predominance of a tonality gives them a certain resemblance to a *Durchführung*. In some of them, Fantasies and Rhapsodies for instance, a tonal centre may be absent in spite of the establishment of certain regions, because in its tonality the harmony is modulatory or even roving.

Introductions, on the other hand, approach the tonic region, at least at their ends. This is definitely true in the Andante, Adagio, etc., introductions to the Allegro, Presto, etc., first movements in Haydn's and Mozart's symphonies. Their modulations, seldom going beyond the regions of classes 1 and 2, are, frequently carried out by sequences, even in roving sections. Whether or not they begin in the tonic region, they certainly end on an " upbeat " harmony [i.e. preparatory dominant].

Haydn: G major Symphony (6): Introduction

155.

Mozart: String Quartet in C major, Introduction

156.

Beethoven's introductions, like everything this great tone-poet created, immediately express part of the drama to follow. The introduction to the Leonora Overture No. 3 (Ex. 157) starts with a descending scale, passing in unison through all the tones of C major. In spite of this, every one of the four measures exhibits a multiple harmonic meaning comparable to that produced by roving vagrants; therefore, the dominant 7th chord on F♯ (mss. 5–6) can introduce the minor triad on B. The following triad on G (ms. 8) is the first distinct expression of C major, but does not introduce the tonic; instead it turns to ♭**SM** (ms. 9), in which there is an episode of six measures. A roving segment leads to a short segment in **m** (ms. 17) which is then followed by **t** (ms. 24). The harmony on A♭ in ms. 27, though introduced by a dominant, is best considered here as VI of **t**, which in ms. 31 is changed to **T**.

Beethoven: Leonora Overture No. 3: Introduction

The introduction to the First Symphony is noteworthy because of its beginning on the subdominant. This and also the introduction to the Second Symphony (Ex. 158) do not go very far afield. The introduction to the Fourth Symphony (Ex. 159), after an introduction of 17 measures in **t**, moves in a somewhat roving manner through **SMm**, **S/T**, **mD**—all classified as ⑤—and **m**. The abrupt return from the unison A to V of **T** is very dramatic.

Beethoven: Symphony No.2 (D major), Introduction

Beethoven: Symphony No.4 (B♭), Introduction

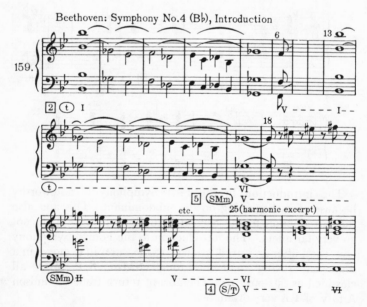

The introduction to the Seventh Symphony[1] (Ex. 160), though fairly long, does not modulate very far, that is, only to ♭**M** and ♭**SM**, classified as ②.

Beethoven: Symphony No. 7 (A major), Introduction

---

[1] This introduction is marked Poco Sostenuto (♩=69). I am convinced that this is a misprint. Evidently the two episodes on ♭**M** and ♭**SM** have a marchlike character. If ♩=69 seems too fast I would suggest ♩=52–54. Besides, if one of these masters writes 16th notes he means it; he means not eighth notes, but fast notes, which will always be heard if the given metronome mark is obeyed.

The introduction to the first movement of the String Quartet
Op. 59/3 is entirely roving. The same is true of the introduction
to the last movement of Op. 18/6 called *La Malinconia* (Ex. 161).

Mendelssohn's and Schumann's introductions do not move
into such remote regions as Beethoven's. Harmonically they
differ from established procedures by a more frequent use of
substitutes and very short deviations into closely related
regions, repetitions of which they do not even avoid.

One of the few introductions in the instrumental works
of Brahms, that to the first movement of the First Symphony
(Ex. 162), must be classified as employing enriched harmony.
At least it does not abandon the tonic region for any length
of time. The introduction to the last movement of the Piano
Quintet (Ex. 163) is even richer in substitutes and transformations, and the quasi-sequential treatment of some phrases
might even suggest the presence of more remote regions.
But a correct analysis will consider most of this introduction
as being in **sd**; it will deny a functional meaning to some of
the harmonies (marked +) whose roving effect derives from the
chromatic (melodic) movement of the main motive.

Brahms: C minor Symphony Introduction

162.

Brahms: Piano Quintet, Introduction, 4th movement

The name Rhapsody suggests an improvisatory construction. When Bach wrote his *Musical Offering* he made clear the difference between an improvisation and an elaborated composition. Though he was a great improviser he could not do justice to a theme given by Frederick the Great. The excellence of an improvisation lies in its inspired directness and liveliness rather than in its elaboration. Of course the difference between a written and an improvised composition is the speed of production, a relative matter. Thus, under fortunate conditions, an improvisation may possess the profundity of elaboration of a carefully worked-out composition. Generally an improvisation will adhere to its subject more through the exercise of imagination and emotion than of the strictly intellectual faculties. There will be an abundance of themes and contrasting ideas whose full effect is achieved through rich modulation, often to remote regions.[1] The connection of themes of such disparate characters and the control over the centrifugal tendency of the harmony is often achieved only in an incidental manner by local " bridges " and even by abrupt juxtapositions.

Brahms' three Rhapsodies for Piano—Op. 79/1 and 2 (Ex. 164) and Op. 119—differ from this description only because of a certain similarity with sonata or rondo forms, the recapitulations in which seemed essential to the organizing mind of Brahms; even an improvisation should not lack such formal balance. Ex. 164 shows the modulatory constitution of the G minor Rhapsody. Clearly it is not only the enriched harmony but also the deviation into many regions which is characteristic here.

Brahms: Rhapsody in G minor, Op.79

---

[1] But why should a musician's brain not work as fast and profoundly as that of a calculating or chess genius?

Liszt's Rhapsodies are looser in construction than those of Brahms. Most of them are also much simpler in modulation and do not move further than Classes 1 and 2. Only Nos. 9 and 14 of the rhapsodies move to regions of Class 5. No. 9 in Eb (Ex. 165) moves (in the Finale) through **SD** to **SDbSM** ⑤, later returning in several steps to **T**. No. 14 in F minor (Ex. 166) moves through **T** to ♯**SM** ④, the signature of two sharps indicating D major, but it seems uncertain whether the D major on which it ends is not a dominant. In this case it would also be questionable whether the repetition in four sharps is really in E major, the E being rather a dominant of the following region, ♯**m**. These endings on dominants may be due to modal influences in Hungarian folksongs, to which evaluation of regions does not apply.

Liszt: Hungarian Rhapsody No.9 (Eb)

Liszt: Hungarian Rhapsody No.14 (f minor)

166.

In some inferior examples of rhapsodies, the title merely gives an excuse for abrupt jumps from one subject to another and from one region to another, for superficial relationships and loose connections, and for total absence of elaboration.

However great the difference between rhapsodies and fantasies may be in aesthetic respects, it can be disregarded from the standpoint of structural functions. Generally rhapsodies attempt to please the listener with the beauty and number of their melodies, while fantasies enable the player to show his brilliancy, and so contain much effective passage work rather than an abundance of beautiful themes.

The lowest forms of organization are the pot-pourri-like Fantasies and Paraphrases. Fortunately these are out of fashion today, though, in my youth, they familiarized one even with good music—for instance, melodies from Mozart's *Don Juan* or *Magic Flute*, Weber's *Freischütz*, Verdi's *Trovatore* and even Wagner's *Tannhäuser*, etc. For that reason I keep a certain gratitude for them.

The following three artistically high-ranking examples of fantasies show similarities as well as divergencies: Bach's Chromatic Fantasy and Fugue (Ex. 167), Mozart's Fantasy in C (Ex. 168) and Beethoven's Fantasy Op. 77 (Ex. 169) (curiously called " in G minor ", though not more than the first three measures are in this tonality). Mozart's fantasy resembles Bach's in its chromaticism; it resembles Beethoven's in its use of many contrasting ideas in the regions which are established. Bach's, on the other hand, is to a great extent

roving, and in the few places where he remains in a region—
the Recitative section—he does not formulate a theme. Even
these regions are expressed merely by 7th and diminished
7th chords of a V followed by a I, which qualifies them as
resting points in an otherwise roving harmony. The beginning
and ending are unquestionably established in D minor.

Bach: Chromatic Fantasy and Fugue

Mozart repeats at the end, in such a way as to establish C minor, the motive which roved in the beginning. This is the only reason for considering C minor as the tonal centre. According to this analysis, almost all of the following regions are remote, connected by roving segments. The regions in which he stays for shorter or longer periods are **m** ③, **msm** ⑤, **msmM=S/T** ⑤, **♯sm** ④, **v** ①, **SD** ③, **sd** ①, **subT** ④, and **v**. Such modulatory movement contradicts a tonal centre even more than a *Durchführung* does.

Mozart: Fantasia

168.

Beethoven's is an extremely "fantastic" fantasy. The concluding section, 83 of the total of 239 measures, a third of the whole piece, consists of a theme and seven variation and a coda in B major, preceded by a Presto introduction of 68 measures in B minor. Thus more than 150 measures are in B major/minor. One could consider the 156 measures which precede the theme and variations in B major as an introduction and call the piece " Introduction and Theme and Variations ", were it not for the considerable number of themes whose appearance is too independent for an introduction. All this suggests basing the analysis on B major as if it were the tonal centre of the piece. The regions would then be: ♭**sm** ③, followed by a sequence in **S/Tm** ⑤ introducing **S/T** ④, and then ♭**smM** ⑤, ♭**m** ③, **SM** ②, and finally **t** and **T**. This analysis is very artificial and rather serves to demonstrate the absence of a tonal centre.

Beethoven: Phantasie, Op.77

169.

The Recitative can be described similarly. The so-called accompanied recitative repeats some phrases occasionally. In the secco recitative, in which roving harmony is the driving power, even such repetitions are lacking. The question as to which features here produce the logic and coherence so necessary for comprehension cannot be answered by an harmonic analysis. Here it is probably the amalgamation of tones with words whose meaning and logic are substitutes for the meaning and logic of tonal progressions.

In the following examples, illustrations of recitatives are analysed from Bach's *St. Matthew Passion*, No. 30 ("Und er kam zu seinem Jüngern") (Ex. 170), Mozart's *Marriage of Figaro* (Act III, preceding the Count's Aria) (Ex. 171), and Beethoven's *Fidelio* (to Leonora's Aria, Act I) (Ex. 172). All three combine secco with accompanied recitative. Again the tonality upon which the evaluation is based is not a real tonal centre but serves only to measure the compass of the regions through which the recitatives move. Bach's recitative follows an Aria in G minor, beginning on the VII of that key. It moves over **dor** ④, to **♯sm** ④. finally arriving at **♯m** ④.

Mozart's recitative begins in the key of C major, to which the following analysis refers. It moves through **M** ②, **S/Tm** ⑤, **S/T** ④, **D** ①, and again **S/T**. Beethoven's recitative passes, with reference to G minor, through the regions of **D**, **♯sm** and **♯SM** ④.

Bach: Matthew Passion: Recitative (No. 30)

Mozart: Marriage of Figaro, Act 3, Recitative

Beethoven: Fidelio, Act I, Recitative, Leonora ("Abscheulicher! wo eilst du hin?")

An attempt to analyse the relations of tonality within an entire opera or at least a single act would not produce any different result. Besides, it is known that composers of operas very often replaced or omitted pieces or even scenes. Though here, too, one could put the responsibility for the structural logic upon the text and the drama, one must admit that the problem of the extent to which an opera is an homogeneous structure has not yet been resolved.

It is difficult to believe that the sense of form, balance and logic of those masters who produced the great symphonies should have been renounced in controlling their dramatic structures.

# CHAPTER XII

EPOCHS in which the venture of experimentation enriched the vocabulary of musical expression have always alternated with their counterparts, epochs in which the experiences of the predecessors were either ignored or else abstracted into strict rules which were applied by the following generations. Most of these rules restricted modulations and designed formulae regarding the inclusion and treatment of dissonances.

These restrictions purported to facilitate the understanding of music. In earlier epochs, even more than in our times, the inclusion of a dissonant tone—" foreign " to the harmony—interrupted plain, undeviating understanding. " Whence comes this tone? Whither does it go?"—these questions distracted the mind of a listener, and could even make him forget the ·basic conditions upon which the continuation of the musical thought depended. Similar disturbances could be caused by the addition of an unexpected chord which was not in accordance with existing conventions. This may have been the reason why, for instance, V–VI in a cadence, instead of V-I, is called a " deceptive " progression. Difficulties of comprehension were once attributed to the minor third. It was at best considered an imperfect consonance, if not a dissonance; accordingly it was considered incapable of producing a definite ending to a work.

Classical music was composed in one of the Apollonian[1] periods, when the application of dissonances and their treatment, as well as the manner and extent of modulation, were governed by rules which had become the second nature of every musician. His musicianship was in question if he failed in this respect, if he were incapable of remaining instinctively within the limits of accepted convention. At this time the harmony was inherent in the melody.

But the new chords and dissonances of the next epoch, a

---

[1] Nietzsche establishes a contrast between the Apollonian mind which aims for proportion, moderation, order and harmony and its contrast, the Dionysian which is passionate, intoxicated, dynamic, expansive, creative, and even, destructive.

Dionysian period (provoked by the romantic composers), had barely been digested and catalogued, and the rules for their inclusion had not yet been formulated, when a new progressive movement began even before this last one had settled down. Mahler, Strauss, Debussy and Reger cast new obstacles in the way of the comprehensibility of music. However, their new and more violent dissonances and modulations could still be catalogued and explained with the theoretical tools of the preceding period.

It is different in the contemporary period.

Because of the many attempts to connect the past with the future one might be inclined to call this an Apollonian period. But the fury with which addicts of various schools fight for their theories presents rather a Dionysian aspect.

Many contemporary composers add dissonant tones to simple melodies, expecting thus to produce " modern " sounds. But they overlook the fact that these added dissonant tones may exert unexpected functions. Other composers conceal the tonality of their themes through harmonies which are unrelated to the themes. Semi-contrapuntal imitations— fugatos taking the place of sequences, which were formerly used as " fillers-up " in worthless " Kapellmeistermusik "— deepen the confusion in which the meagreness of ideas is lost to sight. Here the harmony is illogical and functionless.

My school, including such men as Alban Berg, Anton Webern and others, does not aim at the establishment of a tonality, yet does not exclude it entirely. The procedure is based upon my theory of " the emancipation of the dissonance." Dissonances, according to this theory, are merely more remote consonances in the series of overtones[1]. Though the resemblance of the more remote overtones to the fundamental tone gradually diminishes, their *comprehensibility* is equal to the *comprehensibility* of the consonances. Thus to the ear of today their sense-interrupting effect has disappeared. Their emancipation is as justified as the emancipation of the minor third was in former times.

For the sake of a more profound logic, the Method of Composing with Twelve Tones derives all configurations [elements of a work] from a basic set (*Grundgestalt*) [tone-row

[1] See Arnold Schoenberg: *Harmonielehre*, p. 459ff.

or note-series]. The order in this basic set and its three derivatives—contrary motion [inversion], retrograde, and retrograde inversion respectively—is, like the motive [in classical music], obligatory for a whole piece. Deviation from this order of tones should normally not occur, in contrast to the treatment of the motive, where variation is indispensable.[1] Nevertheless, variety is not precluded. The tones in the right order may appear either successively in a melody, theme or independent voice, or as an accompaniment consisting of simultaneous sounds (like harmonies).

Evaluation of (quasi-) harmonic progressions in such music is obviously a necessity, though more for the teacher than for the composer. But as such progressions do not derive from roots, harmony is not under discussion and evaluation of structural functions cannot be considered. They are vertical projections of the basic set, or parts of it, and their combination is justified by its logic. This occurred to me even before the introduction of the basic set, when I was composing *Pierrot Lunaire*, *Die Glückliche Hand* and other works of this period. Tones of the accompaniment often came to my mind like broken chords, successively rather than simultaneously, in the manner of a melody.

There exists no definition of the concepts of *melody* and *melodic* which is better than mere pseudo-aesthetics. Consequently, the composition of melodies depends solely on inspiration, logic, sense of form and musical culture. A composer in the contrapuntal period was in a similar situation with respect to harmony. Rules give only negative advice, that is, what one must *not* do. He, too, therefore, learned what to do only through inspiration. Is then a composer with twelve tones at a greater disadvantage than his predecessors because the evaluation of the chords which he produces has not yet been carried out?

Theory must never precede creation: " And the Lord saw that all was well done."

One day there will be a theory which abstracts rules from these compositions. Certainly, the structural evaluation of

---

[1] Minor changes in the order are admissible if, because of many repetitions, the mind has become acquainted with the basic set. This corresponds to remote variations of a motive in similar circumstances.

these sounds will again be based upon their functional poten-
tialities. But it is improbable that the quality of sharpness or
mildness of the dissonances—which, in fact, is nothing more
than a gradation according to lesser or greater beauty—is the
appropriate foundation for a theory which explores, explains
and teaches. From such gradations one cannot deduce principles of construction. Which dissonances should come first?
Which later? Should one begin with the sharp ones and end
with the mild ones, or vice-versa? Yet the concept of "first " or
" later " plays a role in musical construction, and " later "
should be the consequence of " first ".

Beauty, an undefined concept, is quite useless as a basis for
aesthetic discrimination, and so is sentiment. Such a " Gefühls-
aesthetik " [aesthetic of sentiment] would lead us back to the
inadequacy of an obsolete aesthetic which compared sounds
to the movement of the stars, and deduced virtues and vices
from tone combinations.

This discussion would fail in its main purpose if the
damage wreaked by the performer's ignorance of the functions
of harmony were to remain undiscussed.

Listening to a concert, I often find myself unexpectedly
in a " foreign country ", not knowing how I got there; a
modulation has occurred which escaped my comprehension.
I am sure that this would not have happened to me in former
times, when a performer's education did not differ from a
composer's.

Great conductors like Nikisch, Mahler and Strauss were
aware of the gradual alteration in the texture which precedes
a modulation and results in a " change of scenery ", the
introduction of a contrast. A musician's culture and sense
of form is acquired by a thorough education and knowledge.
Such a musician will make a modulation lucid by " vitalizing "
the appropriate voices. Then the listener will not awake
suddenly " as in a foreign country ".

Hans Richter, the renowned Wagnerian conductor, was
once passing by a studio in the Vienna Opera House, and
stopped surprised by the unintelligible sounds he heard from
within. A coach who had been engaged for this post, not
because of his musical talents, but because of a powerful
protector, was accompanying a singer. Furiously Richter

opened the door and shouted: " Mr. F---thal, if you plan to continue coaching you must first buy a book on harmony and study it!"

Here was a conductor who believed in harmony and in education.

# GLOSSARY

| *Original* | *Equivalent*<br>(*American or English, where either differs from<br>the original.*) |
|---|---|
| part-leading, voice-leading | part-writing |
| degree | degree of the scale |
| artificial dominant | secondary dominant |
| substitutes, substitutions | borrowed chords, notes |
| transformations | altered chords |
| tone (e.g. leading tone) | note |
| vagrant, roving (harmony) | wandering (i.e. indefinite in key) |
| deceptive (cadence, progression) | false, interrupted |
| half cadence | imperfect cadence |
| cross-relations | false relations |
| flat mediant, flat submediant | flattened mediant, flattened submediant |
| v-minor, five-minor, minor's five | minor chord on dominant (V) |
| registration | indication of region |
| establishing sections | expositions, sections in which tonality is<br>established (see p. 73). |
| *Durchführung* | development, elaboration, working out<br>(see p. 145) |
| measure, measures (ms, mss.) | bar, bars |
| half note | minim |
| quarter note | crotchet |
| eighth note | quaver |
| sixteenth note | semiquaver |
| 6-chord | $\frac{6}{3}$ chord |
| 2-chord | $\frac{4}{2}$ chord |

# TABLE OF DEGREES

(Cf. Chart of the Regions, p. 20)

| Degree | Name | Symbol in Major | Symbol in Minor |
|---|---|---|---|
| I | Tonic | **T** | **t** |
| II | Supertonic | **S/T** | **dor** |
| III | Mediant | **M** | **m** |
| IV | Subdominant | **SD** | **sd** |
| V | Dominant | **D** | **v** |
| VI | Submediant | **SM** | **sm** |

*N.B.* VII, usually called Leading Tone, is not referred to by Schoenberg as a " region-creating " degree in itself; the flat VII in minor he calls Subtonic (SubT)—cf. p. 30.

Flat II is called Neapolitan (Np).

The page references to Schoenberg's *Harmonielehre* apply to the 3rd German Edition (Vienna, 1921); and to the English translation, *Theory of Harmony* (New York, 1948).

# APPENDIX

p. 17: Example 31a — additional examples.

p. 17: Example 31b — additional examples.

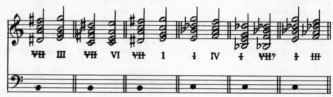

p. 31: In many cases, Transformations and Vagrant Harmonies are used. See Chapters V and VI.

p. 57: Flat Mediant Minor and Flat Submediant Minor are actually classified as "Indirect"; see p. 68.

p. 62: Both "Indirect but Close" and "Indirect" relationships are considered here. See Classification of Regions in Minor, p. 75.

# INDEX OF NAMES

# INDEX OF TERMS